CANCEL THIS!

JONATHAN C. BRENTNER

Author of *The Triumph of the Redeemed*

CANCEL THIS!

What Today's Church Can Learn From

THE BAD GUYS OF THE BIBLE

DEFENDER
CRANE, MO

CANCEL THIS!
What Today's Church Can Learn from the Bad Guys of the Bible
By Jonathan C. Brentner

To my wonderful wife, Ruth: for her amazing kindness, loving support, and encouragement, without which this book would not have been possible.

To my friend Ben Ward, who now resides in Heaven. I'm still encouraged by his boldness, unflinching faith in the face of much adversity, unwavering hope in the Rapture, and humorous way of looking at life.

ACKNOWLEDGMENTS

David Darner, whose enthusiasm for this book prompted me to pursue its publication.

Joe Horn and his amazing staff at SkyWatchTV who have become such an integral part of marketing my books.

Drew Graffia at SkyWatchTV, who encouraged me to submit the book to Defender, which later resulted in its publication.

Angie Peters for her superb job of editing this book and making it more readable.

CONTENTS

IT'S ALL ABOUT WALKING WITH GOD

I wanted to run as far away from the Lord and His Church as possible. Back then, over thirty-five years ago, I hadn't yet learned what it meant to trust God through all the varied heartaches and afflictions of life, even though I had been a believer since age seven and a pastor for six years. When grievous circumstances turned my life upside-down and inside-out, I panicked. Rather than trust the Lord's purposes for my life, I became angry with Him. I remained focused on my temporal aspirations rather than eternal realities.

"If God is good," I said to myself, "why has He allowed so much pain and brokenness to come my way?" Life hadn't turned out the way I had planned, to say the least, and I blamed the Lord for the dreadful turn of events and my continuing sorrow.

Why had He abandoned me after I had worked so hard through college and seminary, then at the two churches where I had served as pastor? Why had He deserted me in the midst of that unending nightmare?

For a while, I kept up a pretense of faithfulness, but my heart remained far from the Lord. I knew Jesus was who He claimed to be: He was my risen Savior. I had no doubts about His Resurrection and the truth of the Gospel message, but I resisted trusting Him with my future. I doubted His unfailing love for me when I needed reassurance of it the most. And, sadly, I questioned His goodness.

The Lord showed up about five years later. After listening to my self-centered prayers during a long run one day, He spoke to the futility of my resistance and asked me to trust Him once again. I accepted His invitation and experienced a renewed closeness to Him, something I hadn't felt for several years prior to that day. (I describe the Lord's life-changing intervention in the introduction to chapter 1.)

I later led a Bible study that I titled "Biblical Characters That Fell Short." The Lord used my preparation for that series to begin a lengthy process of healing my heart from the wounds left by the turbulent events of my past.

During the time I led this study and afterward, I found myself drawn to King Saul; in many ways I saw myself in him. Like Saul, I had allowed pride to manifest itself in my life far too many times. As a pastor, I longed more for the appearance of success than for a close relationship with the Lord. My worship became a means to an end rather than genuine devotion flowing from a heart totally dependent on Jesus and His never-failing love.

When I studied the other biblical figures, I saw how many of them, too, allowed feelings such as pride, anger, resentment, bitterness, revenge, unforgiveness, greed, and discontentment to dominate their relationships with others and with God. As a result, life didn't end well for many of them; some experienced tragedies as they felt the impact of the Lord's judgment. In contemplating the varied outcomes of letting negative emotions control our decisions, I realized it's a whole lot better to trust the Lord, wait for His deliverance from pain, and learn to rest in His love.

The men in this book, except for one notable exception (see chapter

13), ruined their lives because they grew impatient with the Lord, did not trust Him, or both. They cherished personal justice, riches, power, or fame instead of believing the Lord had something better for them— in this life and in eternity. As a result, they made disastrous decisions.

My Purpose for Writing

My purpose for writing this book is not merely to enable you to avoid the blunders of those whose lives we'll be studying, but to guide you as you grow in your relationship with the Lord. Most of the men in this study were familiar with Scripture; they understood how it applied to their lives. Most *never* knew, however, what it meant to truly know the Lord as Savior or how to walk with Him through storms, sorrows, and disappointments.

Christianity is *not* a matter of having good morals or living a disciplined life based on the teachings of the Bible. *It's so much more than that.* It's getting to know Jesus personally through His Word and trusting His purposes for our lives, even when He takes us down paths filled with fierce storms and situations that appear impossible. It's learning to rely upon the promises of Scripture when the road ahead appears daunting and dangerous.

John Eldredge, in his book *Waking the Dead*, writes about the difference between mastering guidelines for living versus developing intimacy with the Lord. Systems of morals or religions can provide "*principles* for a better life," he says. "But only Christianity can teach you to walk with God."[1] The necessity of such a day-by-day dependence on Him, as Eldredge explains, comes from realizing the impossibility of mastering "enough principles to see you safely through this Story.... There are too many surprises, ambiguities, exceptions to the rule."[2]

Living by a list of "do's and don'ts" leads to frustration, doubt, and despair. Approaching the Christian faith in such a way will not give us peace when circumstances threaten to undo us, as they will at times.

Principles alone can't provide guidance when the way before us seems foreboding and dangerous to our well-being as well as to that of those we love.

Only by walking with the Lord daily and relying upon His Word can we hope to navigate all of life's many twists and turns. If we look just at what we can see in front of us, our situations rarely make any sense. Only in light of a Christ-centered perspective that extends far beyond this moment and into eternity can we hope to find any meaning in our diverse experiences as we journey through this vale of tears.

When I think of the years I served as a pastor and afterward, Eldredge's words ring true. I had reduced my faith to a focus on how I was supposed to live and how God ought to respond (by blessing me). I treated the Lord as a vending machine: If I put in the correct amount of change and pressed the right button, I could count on the outcome I desired. When my life went far, far off the tracks, I panicked. God no longer fit inside the box I had put Him in.

I knew better than to place my ultimate dreams on earthly outcomes, but I foolishly thought the Lord owed me something because of my past faithfulness. Even though I loved teaching about prophecy as a young pastor, my eternal focus had become blurred by my worldly aspirations. I held tightly to my earthbound goals, and as a result, I lost sight of my everlasting inheritance and my joyous anticipation in Jesus' imminent appearing.

The "bad guys" in this study lived with a temporal perspective, one that values the things of this life far above the specifics of our eternal hope. Because they lost sight of the glories ahead, they allowed negative emotions to lead them into making disastrous decisions that, in many cases, ruined their lives.

The biblical men we'll be looking at—from noble kings to lowly servants, from faithful fathers to errant sons—had ideas of how God *should* reward them in the here and now. None of them were atheists; all believed in God's existence. However, when things didn't go as they desired or planned, they rebelled. Without true intimacy with the Father and a focus on eternity, they turned away from Him and rejected His authority as well as His purposes for them.

Cancelling God's Ways

Many of the men in this study believed they could find fulfillment apart from the Lord. Driven by earthly desires and unrestrained emotions, they pursued contentment in the things of this world with a perspective limited to the things they could see and obtain.

Many today take their examples to further extremes by seeking to "cancel" what the Lord says about marriage, gender, and morality. Sadly, this effort to dismiss the authority of Scripture has entered many churches.

David Fiorazo, author and founder of the *Stand Up for the Truth* radio program ministry, wrote the following in his book, *Canceling Christianity*:

Practically every survey and cultural indicator reveals we [Christians] have conformed to the world and shows a general failure of the church to disciple and equip believers. Too many Christians are complacent, confused, and disengaged. Some are not even saved! High numbers of young people have left the faith and we now see moral relativism on steroids in our society.[3]

The counter-cultural message of this book strikes back at the wide-spread effort to scrub all of God's ways from our society. No, the pages that follow don't present a battle plan for opposing the cancel culture. Rather, I write about how living out the truths of the Gospel impacts our lives as well as the lives of others in the Body of Christ. The addition of our glorious hope, the future tense of the Gospel, brings amazing peace even in the midst of these perilous times.

Opponents of the Christian faith offer freedom from all restraints in their efforts to cancel all the Lord says about marriage, gender, and the sanctity of life. Those who follow their path resemble what we will see in the upcoming chapters: They live for satisfaction in this life alone, with no thought of eternity.

Satan actively works through his minions to negate biblical standards, but he can't take away the impact of men and women living out the truths of the Gospel. That's where we start in fighting back against the cancel culture that has invaded so many churches.

Walking With God

I conclude each chapter with a "Walking with God" section. These paragraphs focus on what each man we look at teaches us about walking with the Lord through the vast and varied experiences and storms of this life, and will help us avoid repeating their foolish choices that yield disastrous outcomes.

More times than not, these "Walking with God" sections will draw you back to the truths of the Gospel and what Scripture teaches about dealing with the types of issues that have hampered humanity from biblical times to the day in which we're now living.

It's not that the desires these men felt were all wrong, but their emotions, when unrestrained, kept them from a relationship with God. For those of us who are now enjoying fellowship with Him, they can also hinder us in our journey through life.

Beginning Your Walk with God

If you've never entered a saving relationship with Jesus, please do so before it's too late. Cain, one subject in our study, believed in God's existence. How couldn't he? He had audible conversations with Him!

Tragically, however, Cain never knew the Lord as his Savior. He held tightly to his rebellious spirit, seeing no need to be forgiven of his sins. He didn't believe the Lord had anything better for him than what he could get for himself.

Please allow the Holy Spirit to speak to your heart. Don't be like Cain and ignore God's voice calling you to repent of your sins and put your trust solely in the saving work of the Lord Jesus upon the cross. John 3:16 says: "For God so loved the world, that he gave his only Son, that whoever believes in him should not perish but have eternal life." Jesus died in our place so we might receive eternal life rather than perish and endure an eternity without Him.

It's not complicated. Jesus said simply believe in Him and you will receive eternal life. The Apostle Paul, in Romans 10:13, said, "For everyone who calls on the name of the Lord will be saved." If you've never called out to the Lord in faith, please do so today.

Many people of our day follow Cain's example; they know many things about Jesus and perhaps admire His teachings, but they reject His offer of forgiveness for their sins. Instead, they depend on themselves, on their own way of approaching God. They mistakenly think they can bypass Jesus and still get to Heaven based on their own goodness, sincerity, or generic belief in God.

They cannot.

In John 14:6 Jesus said, "I am the way, and the truth, and the life. No one comes to the Father except through me."

Saving faith is exclusive; Jesus is the only path to eternal life.

Is Jesus your Savior? Do you trust Him alone for eternal life? If so, you've already taken the first and most critical step in avoiding the tragic mistakes made by many of the men we'll be studying.

We'll begin by taking a look at King Saul, who, through his failures, teaches about the importance of waiting on the Lord—even when escape seems impossible. Through my study of this king, I discovered a strategy for waiting that brought a calm to my soul during times when I thought God had forgotten about me.

1

SAUL
THE KING WHO DIDN'T WAIT

Those who do not hope cannot wait; but if we hope for that we
see not, then do we with patience wait for it.

—CHARLES SPURGEON

With each step I took, I begged the Lord to intervene on my behalf. I had waited long enough; it was time for my financial situation to improve. Surely God would listen to my desperate, repeated cries for help.

I had recently been interviewed for a promotion at work and was sure getting it represented the answer to my monetary woes. As I awaited the decision of the hiring manager, I spent my late-afternoon five-mile runs pleading with the Lord to give me the position I earnestly desired.

Then something unexpected happened. One day, God showed up toward the end of my run and changed my entire outlook on my past. My self-centered imploring of Him to improve my economic well-being switched to a prayer that sounded something like this: "Lord, I have been through so many years of disappointment, pain, and turmoil. Surely You must have a purpose for all I've endured. I still want this job, but after shedding so many tears all these years, I don't want to miss Your plan for my life, even if it means losing out on this career advancement. I want what You want."

Rather than attempting to force the Lord to take action, I had *finally* reached the place of entrusting Him with my future. Once I said I wanted what *He* wanted for my life, I felt closer to Him than I had in a very long time. Although my waiting on the Lord did not end (I didn't get the job), I look back on that day as a significant turning point in my walk with Jesus.

King Saul, the first biblical figure in our study, reflected the same impatience I exhibited before God interrupted my run that day. When confronted with a dangerous and impossible situation, Saul foolishly plunged ahead without waiting for the Lord. As we will see, while the king's sacrifice appeared to be made with pious motives, it reflected both disobedience and a lack of faith.

We learn many things about waiting from King Saul's example. This insight, however, doesn't come from his godly character but from his failure in all the tests the Lord put before him.

The excuses he offered after one of his disobedient acts provide valuable lessons on how we can avoid the pitfalls of misguided reasoning that leaves out dependence upon the Lord.

Before we examine Saul's feeble attempts to explain his ill-fated decision, let's look at Israel's ominous situation as a large and well-armed Philistine army assembled and prepared to attack the much smaller nation (1 Samuel 13).

The king had valid reasons to be afraid; his situation looked bleak, at best.

It's Impossible

The account we're looking at on this occasion begins with a bold and successful attack by Jonathan, Saul's son, on the Philistine outpost at Geba (1 Samuel 13:3). King Saul announced the victory to Israel (albeit by taking credit for the accomplishment himself), hoping it would rally his soldiers to fight against their long-time foe (vv. 3–4). It didn't. The number of soldiers remaining with him dwindled from three thousand down to six hundred (1 Samuel 13:2, 15).

The Philistines, on the other hand, had no problem putting together a large and fierce fighting force. First Samuel 13:5 says they had "thirty thousand chariots and six thousand horsemen and troops like the sand on the seashore in multitude." This demonstration of power understandably struck fear in the hearts of the Israelites.

Instead of joining Saul, the "men of Israel" hid in caves, in holes (or pits), behind rocks, or anywhere else they could find protection (1 Samuel 13:6). Some crossed to the other side of the Jordan River (1 Samuel 13:7). Later, we discover that potential Israeli soldiers even went over to the side of the Philistines until Israel gained the upper hand (1 Samuel 14:21).

Afterward, it got even worse for the king. First Samuel 13:19–22 reveals that, on the day of battle, only Saul and Jonathan had a sword or spear. The Philistines had earlier taken away Israel's blacksmiths to keep the Hebrews from making such weapons. The Israelites thus needed to rely on clubs, slingshots, and crude bows and arrows to fight against the warriors on chariots and a huge Philistine army that actually possessed swords, spears, and bows with metal-tipped arrows.

No wonder so many of the Israelites chose to hide rather than join Saul and fight against such a well-armed enemy. What good were clubs against swords and chariots? How could they even hope to prevail with so few weapons?

Previously, God had told King Saul to wait seven days for the prophet Samuel to arrive to offer a sacrifice and tell Saul what to do (1 Samuel 10:8). While this initial command for Saul to wait appears to have been at the beginning of his reign, 1 Samuel 13:8 reveals the king clearly understood that he needed to wait seven days for the prophet on this occasion as well.

What was the significance of Samuel arriving to offer this sacrifice?

Earlier, in 1 Samuel 7, we read that Israel faced a similar threat from the Philistines. As the Israelites watched their enemy advance, Samuel offered a sacrifice and the Lord put the Philistine army into a panic, leading to a great victory for Israel (1 Samuel 7:5–13).

Saul Doesn't Wait

The delay in Samuel's arrival on this occasion posed a critical test for Saul. Would the king trust the Lord and wait for Samuel, or would he take matters into his own hands?

Saul, seeing his men scatter in response to the Philistine threat, caved to the mounting pressure and offered the sacrifice before the prophet arrived (1 Samuel 13:9–10). When Samuel came shortly thereafter to find smoke still flowing upward from the fire on the altar, the king went out to greet the prophet as though he had done nothing wrong. He didn't understand the significance of his disobedience. After all, he had offered a sacrifice to God; what harm could there possibly be in that?

Some commentators believe Saul's sin was in assuming the role of a priest to present the sacrifice. While that's possible, other passages speak of a king performing that duty when the text assumes one or even a large group of priests were present, such as in 2 Chronicles 7:4–5. Further, Samuel doesn't specifically rebuke the king for acting as a priest, but for disobeying the specific command to wait for him before offering the sacrifice (1 Samuel 13:13).

After listening to Saul's excuses, Samuel told the king he had "acted foolishly" by going against the Lord's instructions. The prophet said that, because of Saul's disobedience, God would choose someone else through whom He would establish a lasting kingdom (1 Samuel 13:13–14).

Samuel left without giving the king any counsel from God regarding the upcoming battle. Surprisingly, Saul didn't try to stop Samuel and plead with him for direction about how to proceed against the Philistines.

A Strategy for Waiting

We all face challenging times when the Lord makes us wait for an answer to a prayer, a way out of a dilemma, or the fulfillment of an urgent need. Our situation may not be as desperate as that of King Saul, but nonetheless we're tempted to run ahead of God to seek our own solutions.

The reasons Saul gave for his disobedience help us understand where his thinking went awry and provide valuable insights as to how we can avoid taking on that faulty perspective. An examination of the king's excuses, in fact, lays out a strategy we can use when God makes us wait, even in the midst of frightening and seemingly impossible situations.

1. Focus on Christ, Not the Mess

Samuel confronted Saul with a simple, yet probing, question on that fateful day: "What have you done?" In response, Saul said, "When I saw that the people were scattering, and that you did not come within the days appointed, and that the Philistines had mustered at Micmash.... I forced myself, and offered the burnt offering" (1 Samuel 13:11–12). As he waited for the prophet's arrival, Saul fixed his attention on his deserting army, Samuel's delay, and the massive force assembling against Israel.

In other words, Saul focused on the mess rather than on the Lord. While his situation was indeed dire, he erred by taking his eyes off of the One who alone could deliver Israel from the Philistines.

We can almost hear Saul calculating and comparing his army to that of the enemy: "How am I going to make this work? How many more men can I afford to lose? I can't let this situation get any more desperate; I have to do something." In light of the Philistine threat, however, no amount of planning or human intervention was going to save him from devastating defeat and certain death.

The king never reached the point where he fully grasped the impossibility of his situation. Even if he had kept all his men, he would have had a mere three thousand unarmed soldiers. On a human level, what could they have done against the thousands of Philistine chariots and a multitude of armed soldiers? Saul sought in vain to hold on to what he had, not fully comprehending the overwhelming odds against him. He didn't see that only the Lord could save him in his current predicament.

Saul didn't understand that, with God, there are no impossible situations. The level of our hopelessness does not limit His ability to solve our problems. His power is infinite. He can deal with our messes, regardless of how overwhelming they seem. As the Lord told the prophet Jeremiah, "Behold, I am the Lord, the God of all flesh. Is anything too hard for me?" (Jeremiah 32:27). The Lord is more than able to deal with any troubling circumstances we face.

An account from the Gospel of Matthew illustrates our need to focus on Christ rather than on our circumstances. When Jesus walked on the water toward His disciples, who were in a boat on the Sea of Galilee, Peter asked if he could walk out to meet Him (Matthew 14:25–28). The Lord told Peter to come, "but when he [Peter] saw the wind, he was afraid, and beginning to sink he cried out, 'Lord, save me'" (Matthew 14:30).

Did you catch that? Peter sank not when he stepped onto the water, but when he took his eyes off Jesus. Isn't this what we often do as well?

Like the apostle, we falter when we allow the dark storm clouds around us to divert our attention from our Lord. When we find ourselves in an impossible situation, that's the time to realize our only hope is in Christ.

The first lesson on waiting that we learn from King Saul's impatience is to fix our eyes on the Lord rather than on the storm raging around us: *Focus on Christ rather than the mess.*

2. Don't Buy into the World's Reasoning

Saul's words in 1 Samuel 13:12 reveal another area where his thinking went far off course: "I said, 'Now the Philistines will come down against me at Gilgal, and I have not sought the favor of the Lord.' So I forced myself, and offered the burnt offering." The king disobeyed because he thought the sacrifice itself would prevent more troops from leaving (see 1 Samuel 13:11) and would help him gain God's favor.

Saul didn't understand the purpose of the sacrifice. It wasn't to secure God's favor; Israel already had that in large measure. Nor was it a time to keep the troops he already had with him. This was to be the time the king would hear Samuel's instructions as the prophet rallied the people to look to the Lord for deliverance.

Saul's excuse revealed his misplaced faith.

Rather than trust God to deliver Israel, Saul put his hope in the offering itself to keep his soldiers from fleeing, to please God, and to rescue the nation from the Philistines. The king relied on the action—the sacrifice—rather than on God, who alone could deliver Israel from the dire threat.

In other words, *Saul believed the ends would justify the means.*

Since the sacrifice would lead to what he believed would be a positive outcome, Saul reasoned that his action was necessary even though he knew it was disobedient to the Lord.

The king did not stop to ask himself how defying the Lord's instruction to wait would help with his impossible situation. He focused solely on the results, no matter how he achieved them.

Such pragmatic reasoning remains popular today. It's common for people to believe that results determine whether actions are right or wrong. If everything turns out okay, many folks believe their behavior must have been the right thing to do. Such thinking, however, ignores the standard established by God's Word. Pursuing positive outcomes never justifies acting contrary to what the Word of the Lord instructs. Instead, it displays devotion to temporal results at the expense of eternal realities.

The standards of right and wrong revealed in Scripture have clearly lost their foothold in our culture. Society openly rebels against the Lord's principles and substitutes shifting values based on the need of the moment, feelings, or the voice of the majority. Such relativism is rampant in our world—as it is, sadly, in most churches as well. Many people, including professing Christians, openly defy God's Word and its values and substitute shifting sentimentality that puts their view of love far above the words of Scripture.

About thirty years ago, Dr. Jeff Gilmore, senior pastor of the church I attended at the time, said something that caught my attention: "In God's way of thinking, success is just as much the process as it is the final outcome." The Lord is just as much interested in our faithfulness during the storm as He is with the final outcome—perhaps even more so. Through our faithfulness, according to Dr. Gilmore, we can become *heroes* in God's sight even before the end of the trials He sends our way.

In the midst of troubling situations, we naturally put our hope on the light at the end of the tunnel; we look forward to the time when our affliction will end. God, however, wants to accomplish much within us *during* the tempest.

Using the reasoning of the world will cause us to copy Saul's behavior as we become increasingly impatient with the Lord and feel tempted to take shortcuts to improve our situation. *What harm is there in cheating on my taxes or in misrepresenting my qualifications to a potential employer?* Such logic, however, ignores the fact that the Lord is just as interested in how our faith holds up *during* the storm as He is with what happens *after* it.

In contrast to the results-oriented Saul, God wants us to become process-oriented people. I must admit this is much easier said than done, but it's something that can greatly encourage us when we're facing daunting challenges.

Hebrews 11:33–34; 36–38 reveals a variety of outcomes for Old Testament heroes who chose to walk by faith. The text says:

> [Some] conquered kingdoms, enforced justice, obtained prom-
> ises, stopped the mouths of lions, quenched the power of flames,
> and escaped the edge of the sword…. Others suffered mocking
> and flogging, and even chains and imprisonment. They were

stoned, they were sawn in two, they were killed with the sword. They went about in skins of sheep and goats, destitute, afflicted, mistreated—of whom the world was not worthy—wandering about in deserts and mountains, and in dens and caves of the earth.

Notice the wide range of results that come from having the same faith in the same Lord. Right in the middle of a sentence, the outcomes switch from conquering kingdoms to being tortured, afflicted, and even martyred.

Who can know where our walk of faith will take us? The Lord, through the writer of Hebrews, honors those the world regards as failures, stating "the world was not worthy of them." God saw their lives as success stories because of their faithfulness during times of tremendous persecution. He didn't lead them out of their tribulations, but instead used their afflictions and even their deaths for His glory. He honored their faith just as much as those who conquered kingdoms—perhaps even more so.

No matter how compelling the world's arguments appear, we must not allow ourselves to run ahead of the Lord and rely on the world's wisdom rather than His. In the end, His answer will not disappoint us. Even though the wait may be distressingly long and painful, we can trust what He might accomplish through our time of waiting. Regardless of the outcome, He sees our devotion and will surely reward us for it.

God is ever so faithful.

3. Hold on to God's Promises

The nightmare seemed vividly real. I dreamed of my life fifteen years in the future, and everything was the same. I was still alone, struggling, and unable to pay all my bills. It appeared as though my current difficult circumstances would continue, with no end in sight! "Is this dream foretelling my future?" I wondered.

The next morning, I determined to go for a long run later in the day and have a heart-to-heart talk with the Lord about my troubling dream. So, once I got back home from work, I did just that. As I started out, I asked Him what the dream signified. Was I really destined to endure turmoil for the indefinite future? Would I really be waiting for years without end?

As I was jogging, the Lord reminded me of a verse I had previously memorized and recited more times than I could count: "I am still confident of this: I will see the goodness of the Lord in the land of the living" (Psalm 27:13, NIV).

As the Spirit brought these words to mind, joy bubbled up inside me. The nightmare was not true; I would see God's goodness in the future despite my current circumstances.

For months, I had held tightly to this verse for encouragement. I'm not sure why I had forgotten it earlier that day, but as the Spirit again made me aware of this promise, I felt great relief. Despite the wait, which would continue for many years after that day, I knew I could count on His goodness. (And now I can say that, after experiencing so much grief, the Lord has poured His goodness into my life in ways that would have staggered my imagination twenty-five years ago.)

Thus, the third lesson we learn from Saul's faulty thinking is this: *We must hold tightly to God's promises.*

The Lord's command for Saul to wait for Samuel contained a promise: When Samuel arrived on the seventh day, he would give the king guidance; the prophet would tell the king what to do in order for God to win the battle for Israel (1 Samuel 10:8). The Lord had a plan to deliver His people from the Philistines, but in his impatience, the king missed it.

Saul had also received another promise he could have relied upon that day. In the process of selecting Saul, the Lord had told Samuel the new king would "save my people from the hand of the Philistines" (1 Samuel 9:16). How could Saul have forgotten this promise? Didn't he trust the Lord and His power to deliver him?

These two pledges from God should have strengthened Saul's resolve as he awaited the prophet's arrival on that fateful day. Yet he ignored both of the assurances the Lord had already given him.

Merely knowing about God's promises is not enough; we must make them personal, cling tightly to them in times of despair, and find ways to repeatedly bring them to our attention. I've found it helpful to write key verses on sticky notes and place them where I will see them often. I had done this with Psalm 27:13 before the Holy Spirit refreshed my memory during my run that day.

There's one more important consideration we must remember while we're in the midst of painful experiences.

4. Trust God's Person, Not "Religious" Behavior

For a long time, I wrestled with another aspect of the excuses Saul offered Samuel. Something else was amiss in his faulty attempt at worship that day, but at first, I couldn't identify it. Then it occurred to me: The king was treating the Lord as a good-luck charm rather than as a living, personal being.

Saul's excuses reveal that he trusted the sacrifice itself for success rather than the One to whom he was making the offering. Saul trusted a religious exercise rather than God to deliver Israel. He didn't consider that victory rested solely with the very One he was disobeying.

Activities such as daily prayer, Bible study, and worship are essential for a close relationship with the Lord, no doubt about it. However, when tragedies and tribulations beset us, it's God, the object of our worship and faith, who provides the strength and encouragement we need to get through them. He alone is able to deliver us from the perils that confront us. He, not our godly behavior, empowers and delivers us as we go through tough times.

When we wait for God rather than run ahead of Him to find our own solutions, we demonstrate that our hope rests solely in His character. We acknowledge that He dearly loves us and wants the best for us, even when we can't see it at the time.

It's never a matter of trading religious behavior for His predictable outcomes. That's what a vending machine does; wouldn't it be boring if God behaved like that? I think so!

The Lord is so much more than a coin-operated machine. Even when the way seems dark, we can fully trust the One who is "able to do far more abundantly than all we ask or think, according to the power at work within us" (Ephesians 3:20). The ultimate blessing of waiting on God is often much better than we could ever expect, even if we don't see what He had planned for us after this life, in Jesus' Kingdom.

Today, I'm exceedingly grateful that the Lord didn't give me the job I begged Him for during my runs so long ago (see the introduction to this chapter). He had a significantly better path in mind for me. Yes, God's track for my future involved more waiting and much additional grief along the way, but the result turned out far better than if He had initially said "yes" to my selfish and shortsighted prayers.

His plan for me has far exceeded all I could have imagined or even asked the Lord for at that time. And I still reside on this side of eternity, where my ultimate hopes and joyous expectations rest. I can't fathom the glory that awaits all of us who know Jesus as Savior.

Walking with God

King Saul helps us understand the offer of true life comes from a loving, personal God who pursues a close relationship with us. He often leads us through difficult circumstances and makes us wait—even when things get much worse, not better. In such cases, we must trust in His love for us, not in ourselves or our good behavior. It's all about learning to remain in His goodness and steadfast love as we make our way through the mire here below.

The Lord has a unique plan for each of us. We all have different personalities, abilities, spiritual gifts, and experiences. God doesn't apply cookie-cutter solutions to our dilemmas, but works in each life according to His distinct purposes. That's why our focus must be on the Lord rather than our situation...or even on how God is working in the life of the person seated next to us at church.

Jesus also has personalized roles for us in His coming Kingdom when He rules over the nations of the world seated on the throne of David. Who knows how our varied experiences might fit into the future places He has for us?

Even if we don't see the resolution to our suffering in the near term, we know a joyous "forever" awaits. God will not disappoint us; His never-ending blessings will be well worth the wait! That's the perspective I lacked during the dark years when I doubted His amazing love for me.

Many of you know all about seemingly impossible circumstances. You may believe you've done all you can—and more. Still, your problems persist, with no solution in sight. You can't imagine holding on much longer. I've been in that situation, and all too slowly I realized that sometimes all I could do is wait.

I am not advocating "do-nothing" approaches to problem-solving. I'm simply pointing out that there will always be times when we find ourselves in predicaments with only one way out: Wait for the Lord.

Even now, as we look forward to the Lord's appearing to take us home, we see the dark clouds of the Tribulation approaching as wickedness, deception, and violence increase exponentially all around us.

"How much longer?" we ask.

I never thought we would see so much evil, corruption, and deceit occurring before the Rapture takes place. However, I know Jesus is coming soon, and He will take us home before the start of the seven-year Tribulation.

In the next chapter, we'll see how Saul's son Jonathan took a step of faith and sent the massive army of the Philistines on the run.

STUDY GUIDE

Chapter 1

Saul: The King Who Didn't Wait

Passage to read: 1 Samuel 13
Key verses: Hebrews 11:33–38; Ephesians 3:20

Questions for discussion:

1. What factors made the predicament for Saul and his army impossible on a human level?
2. Why did most of the men in Israel run and hide as the Philistine threat grew?
3. Why is it important to focus on Christ rather than on the mess around us?
4. How did King Saul imitate the reasoning of the world?
5. What does Hebrews 11:33–38 tell us about what we can expect from a walk of faith?
6. Why is it essential to rely on God's promises during challenging situations or even seemingly impossible circumstances?
7. How would you explain the difference between depending on godly behavior and relying on God Himself?
8. Share a time when God's answer to one of your prayers was "no." Did you later see His wisdom in not agreeing to your request?

STUDY GUIDE

Chapter 1

9. What is the key lesson you've learned from this chapter that will help you maintain a close walk with the Lord?

Key lesson: God doesn't apply cookie-cutter solutions to our dilemmas, but works in each life according to His distinct purpose. That's why our sights must be on the Lord rather than on the predicaments we face or even on how God is working in the lives of those we read about on social media.

Regardless of our situation or pain, our faithfulness will bring Him glory—now and in eternity.

2

SAUL

THE KING WHO COWERED WHILE HIS SON CLIMBED

A proud man is always looking down on things and people;
and, of course, as long as you are looking down, you cannot see
something that is above you.

—C. S. LEWIS, MERE CHRISTIANITY

ric Liddell went to the 1924 Olympics in Paris as the overwhelming favorite to win the gold medal in the 100-meter race. He had won a similar event, the 100-yard dash, during the previous year with a record time of 9.7 seconds. All of his expected competition in the Olympics had failed to break the 10-second mark for that distance.

After Liddell arrived in Paris, he discovered that, in order to compete in the 100-meter event, he would have to run the qualifying heat on a Sunday. Believing strongly that Sundays were to be set aside to honor the Lord, he withdrew from that race and entered the 400-meter event, which wouldn't require him to run on a Sunday to be eligible for the medal race.

Liddell believed putting God first outweighed any personal glory he would get if he did win the gold in the 100-meter race. As a result, he opted to participate in another event that offered him only a remote chance, at best, of winning a gold medal.

As the time came for the 400-meter event, the crowd, well aware of Liddell's decision, fell silent in anticipation. When the gun sounded, Liddell jumped to the lead, running in what one reporter later described as "a most lion-hearted manner." The athlete went as fast as he could throughout the race, finishing with a world-record time of 47.6 seconds. Many consider his victory the greatest achievement in the 1924 Olympics. Sports writers regard it as one of the most memorable events in all of Olympic history.

Liddell chose to honor God rather than go for the personal glory of winning the 100-meter race. The Lord, however, used his decision in a way the runner could never have imagined. With the world watching and well aware of his decision, he won the gold medal in record time. The news media broadcast the account of his triumph after putting God first; that story was later featured in theaters around the world in the wildly popular movie, *Chariots of Fire*.

We find this same God-honoring attitude this athlete had in Jonathan, the son of King Saul. As you might expect, he differed greatly from his father. The king always sought his own glory; he only cared about making himself look good. Jonathan, however, strove to exalt God in all he did.

As we continue to examine Saul's life, we will contrast his self-centeredness against his son's desire to give all the credit for his successes to the Lord. The difference in the character of each man will help us better understand what it means to honor God with our lives.

At the end of chapter 1, we left Saul in a dire predicament. His small and ill-equipped army faced the threat of a large Philistine force that could easily destroy them. After Saul's failure to wait for the prophet Samuel, the king led his army into hiding. His son, however, left the camp to find a way to attack the enemy.

Jonathan's Surprise Attack

Jonathan's surprise attack on the Philistine garrison might at first seem suicidal. Humanly speaking, we might ask, "What was he thinking?" However, as we will see, his action displayed great faith as well as wisdom and courage. First Samuel 14:1–15 provides the details of his valiant assault on the enemy stronghold.

The account begins with Jonathan and his armor-bearer leaving the Israelite camp without telling anyone, especially his father (1 Samuel 14:1–3). Armor-bearers played a vital role in ancient times. They needed to be particularly brave and loyal to their masters. Jonathan's armor-bearer reflected both of these characteristics and, most importantly, he shared his master's faith in God.

Jonathan knew the Philistine army had positioned a detachment at the Michmash Pass to establish a stronghold on top of its high cliffs. He was likely rather familiar with that area since he had grown up in nearby Gibeon (1 Chronicles 9:35, 39).

I believe he knew all about this gorge with its precipices on each side; he had likely climbed them often as a young boy. He understood exactly how to reach the top, where the Philistines had established their garrison. Jonathan used his familiarity with this location to devise a plan to surprise the enemy and gain an advantage.

We see the faith of Jonathan evident in his appeal to his armor-bearer: "Come, let us go over to the garrison of these uncircumcised. It may be that the Lord will work for us, for nothing can hinder the Lord from saving by many or by few" (1 Samuel 14:6). Jonathan's confidence rested in God, not himself. He expected the Lord to do great things for Israel. In contrast to the king, Jonathan believed the Lord could achieve a victory for Israel despite the overwhelming disadvantage.

Verse 6 also reveals Jonathan's perspective on the battle. He regarded the Philistines as God's adversary ("these uncircumcised"). They were foes of both Israel and the Lord. The enemy combatants were not part of God's everlasting covenant with His nation, which meant the territory they occupied did not belong to them. The Lord had *forever* given the land to the descendants of Jacob (see Psalm 105:8–11). The land belonged to Israel!

Jonathan also believed the Lord's promise to defeat the Philistines during his father's reign (see 1 Samuel 9:16). He wasn't content to cower in fear beside his father. Believing the Lord could—and would—conquer Israel's foes, he set out to look for an opportunity to give God a chance to fight for His people. The Lord didn't need many soldiers to triumph over the invaders; perhaps He could use just him and his armor-bearer to accomplish the victory.

Jonathan proposed a way to determine God's will for his strategy. He and his armor-bearer would show themselves to the Philistines. If they invited them up, they would know the Lord was giving them into their hands. If they stated their intent to come down the cliff to meet them, it would be the Lord's sign not to attack (1 Samuel 14:8–10).

This approach employs much common sense. The Philistines' unwillingness to come down and confront the pair would reveal overconfidence on their part as well as a lack of concern about the threat posed by Jonathan and his armor-bearer.

On the other hand, a decision by the combatants to challenge the two face to face would display courage, demonstrate they were still on guard, and eliminate Jonathan's strategy of surprise.

When the Philistines saw the two Israelites, they mockingly invited them to come up, saying, "We will show you a thing," which meant they would teach them a lesson (1 Samuel 14:11–12). They had no doubt heard the reports that Saul's army was cowering in fear, which led to their smug, brash attitude.

This was the reply Jonathan wanted to hear; it told him they could surprise the enemy and the Lord would give them the victory.

"Come up after me, for the Lord has given them into the hand of Israel," Jonathan told his armor-bearer (1 Samuel 14:12). Jonathan's perspective illuminates his faith still further. He didn't fight for himself or to enhance his own reputation. The Lord would deliver the Philistines into the "hand of Israel," not into his own hand. He gave God all the credit for the win even before he took action.

Once Jonathan and his armor-bearer reached the top of the cliff and attacked, the startled Philistines ran for their lives. The pair killed twenty of them as God struck fear into the hearts of those who remained (1 Samuel 14:13–14). The Lord honored Jonathan's faith by using his strategy to put the invaders of Israel into a state of sheer panic.

It helps to see the situation from the vantage point of the Philistines, who had heard the reports of the widespread fear in Israel's camp. They knew most of the Israelite men had gone into hiding rather than fight.

Suddenly, two Israelites appeared in their camp and began attacking them. The enemy soldiers never would have thought that only a pair of soldiers would have the courage to climb up the steep cliff and assault them. The Philistines left in such a hurry they may not have realized that they were running from just two men. And, of course, it was the Lord who was sending them on the run.

As He had so often done during the history of the Israelites, the Lord used the incident to throw the Philistine army into disarray. First Samuel 14:15 says "the earth quaked" as He sent a shockwave of hysteria throughout the ranks of the Philistines. The tumult soon caught the attention of King Saul, who hadn't yet noticed Jonathan was missing.

How would the king respond now that God was clearly giving the enemy into Israel's hands?

Saul's Self-Seeking Response

When reports of the fleeing Philistines reached Saul, he asked the high priest, Ahijah, for help in getting God's direction (1 Samuel 14:18–19). As the commotion in the Philistine camp grew, Saul gave up on waiting for an answer from the Lord and assembled his troops for battle. The king's delay, however, wasted the forces' valuable time before joining the fight against the fleeing enemy.

While it might seem unusual to criticize someone for seeking God's will, I believe Saul did it to draw attention to himself. With the Lord so clearly causing the Philistines to flee, wasn't it foolish for the king to waste even a few seconds trying to discern the Lord's guidance? Who else but the Lord could put tens of thousands of enemy combatants into such a frenzy with only two soldiers? Who else but God could cause the Philistines to forget about their staggering advantage (with their thirty thousand chariots) over the Israelites?

We can understand why the Lord didn't bother to respond to the king's inquiry. Saul already knew the course of action he needed to take.

When the king and his army arrived on the battlefield, they found the Philistines in disarray, fighting among each other. The Lord had brought "very great confusion" upon them. In a situation that had seemed utterly hopeless for Israel hours earlier, He was giving His people a miraculous victory (1 Samuel 14:20–23).

Unfortunately, King Saul's rash and reckless action limited Israel's success that day. First Samuel 14:24 says:

> The men of Israel had been hard pressed that day, so Saul had laid an oath on the people, saying, "Cursed be the man who eats food until it is evening and I am avenged on my enemies." So none of the people had tasted food.

The foolishness of Saul's command soon became apparent. The soldiers needed food to keep up their strength as they chased the fleeing Philistines. In his eagerness to draw attention to himself, the king neglected any semblance of wisdom. How could he expect his troops to pursue the enemy all day without nourishment?

Saul sought to focus all the attention on himself rather than the Lord. For him, it was all about how *he* could avenge *his* enemies. The king wanted *all* the credit for the victory—even though he had remained in hiding until the Lord turned the tide in Israel's favor. Notice the contrast between his behavior and the actions of his son, who regarded the

Philistines as God's enemies and gave Him all the praise for what he anticipated would be a triumph.

Jonathan, busily pursuing the Philistines, didn't hear about Saul's oath until after he had eaten honey (1 Samuel 14:27–28). When he heard about the restriction, he criticized his father's carelessness, saying, "How much better if the people had eaten freely today of the spoil of their enemies that they found. For now the defeat among the Philistines has not been great" (1 Samuel. 14:30). He saw the foolishness behind the vow his father had imposed on his army; it restricted the ability of his soldiers to fight and limited the scope of the victory that day.

An Outlook That Honors the Lord

The contrast between Jonathan and King Saul provides valuable insight on making decisions that honor the Lord, especially in situations that appear impossible. We will focus primarily on Jonathan's example, since his selfless attitude is the exact opposite of his father's self-seeking one. Jonathan's behavior reveals a mindset of faith that can enable us to map out God-honoring strategies for dealing with trials and afflictions that come our way.

What mentality honors the Lord in the midst of difficult circumstances? How can we make decisions that glorify Him?

1. Have Confidence in God's Purposes

Jonathan believed God had an answer to the Israelite army's predicament. His faith led him to look for a way to confront the Philistines. He knew the Lord had a purpose for Israel's crisis and thus a path to victory that would honor Him alone.

Jonathan trusted God to provide the opening the Israelites needed. He believed the covenant promises regarding Israel, and he based his confidence on those promises rather than on his own abilities. He began with the conviction that the Lord had a reason for putting the Israelite army up against great odds and assumed He would give His people great success.

Jonathan's actions proved his great faith in the Lord. Even though Israel's situation was hopeless and bleak, to say the least, Jonathan believed God could and would deliver His people. He never lost confidence in the Lord's enduring purposes for Israel.

Saul, on the other hand, stationed himself in a pomegranate cave (some versions say under a pomegranate tree) after Samuel's rebuke (1 Samuel 14:1–2). He did not seek the Lord's direction regarding his dire situation until after Jonathan's ambush that caused the Philistines to scatter.

One verse that stood out during the many years of waiting I described in chapter 1 was Jeremiah 29:11: "I know the plans I have for you, declares the Lord, plans for welfare and not for evil, to give you a future and a hope." I realize the context of this promise is for Israel and pertains to its future return to the land when the Lord will reign over them. However, I believe we can apply this verse to our lives as well, because it speaks to God's character and His love for all His people. For me, it meant I could trust His reasons for whatever He allowed to come into my life, even though at times I couldn't see or understand them.

Psalm 139:17 says, "How precious to me are your thoughts, O God! How vast is the sum of them!" We can depend on the plans of the One who continually watches over us with unfailing and steadfast love. We can have confidence in Him regardless of what comes our way.

Several years ago, I called my friend Denny the day after he had undergone major cancer surgery on his colon. I wanted to find out how the operation had gone and give him some encouragement. Minutes before my call, the doctors had informed him there was nothing else they could do about his cancer; it had spread too far. They told him he might have six months to live, but no longer than that.

The news shook me more than it did Denny. He relayed the diagnosis to me with a confidence that could only have come from the Lord.

From that point forward, he never wavered in his trust of the Lord's wisdom despite the dire diagnosis. During his final months, Denny often said, "I know where I am going," as he reached out to others and told them about Jesus and His saving message.

Denny saw his impending death as an opportunity to bring attention to the goodness of Christ and share the message of His saving grace to the many unsaved members of his family, especially with his eight brothers. He never felt sorry for himself, but relied on God even as he faced suffering and certain death.

Like Jonathan, Denny exalted the Lord during his final days of battling cancer. He remained confident of God's purposes for his earthly life to its very end. He encouraged other believers, including me, with his calm assurance of spending eternity with the Lord. His favorite song, "I Can Only Imagine," was a highlight of his funeral. He had planned the service so it would herald the good news of salvation and glorify the One he loved so very much.

2. Seek God's Glory, Not Your Own

No matter how many times I read 1 Samuel 14, I'm still amazed by Jonathan's faith and his desire to give the Lord full credit for everything. He saw himself as merely a player in the struggle between God and His adversaries.

Notice his certainty in verse 12: "Come up after me, for the Lord has given them into the hand of Israel." From Jonathan's perspective, the battle was never about obtaining a personal accomplishment; it was always all about God achieving a triumph on behalf of Israel, His people.

Unlike his son, Saul used the occasion to draw attention to himself; he wanted vengeance in order to make himself—not the Lord, the One who was giving Israel the victory—look good (1 Samuel 14:24). With the battle clearly going in Israel's favor, Saul saw an opportunity to grab some personal kudos.

Eric Liddle mirrored Jonathan's attitude when he arrived at the 1924

Olympics. Like Jonathan, he saw the bigger picture; he understood that,
in the end, the battle belonged to the Lord. And the Lord rewarded both
of them for their self-sacrificing faith.

When Liddle gave up what he believed was his only chance for a
gold medal, he could never have imagined that, years later, someone
would produce the wonderful movie, *Chariots of Fire*, to tell the story
of his choice to honor the Lord above personal fame. Likewise, I'm sure
Jonathan never thought it possible that, three thousand years later, we
would be studying his courageous faith, which led to a historic conquest
for Israel.

3. Apply Past Experience to Current Circumstances

Jonathan used childhood memories to help devise his strategy for attacking the Philistines. What made him so confident that he could climb up
the side of the cliff to reach the enemy camp? As stated earlier, I believe
he knew the area and had scaled those bluffs as a youth—perhaps several
times. His past experience told him this plan could succeed if the Lord
gave him the green light.

While we are waiting during times of crisis, one thing we can do is
evaluate our past experiences to recall skills we learned or insights we
gained that might apply to our current circumstances. This doesn't mean
we should give up on trusting the Lord to work, but that we can look for
ways He may have already provided answers to our situation.

Upon receiving my Master of Business (MBA) degree (after my
time as a pastor), I applied for many financial analyst jobs, but nothing
opened up. After a year and a half of waiting and striving without success, my previous seven years of writing for David C. Cook unlocked
the door that led to my career as a senior financial analyst. It came about
after I successfully applied for a job as a technical writer.

While in my role as a writer, a new program manager took over the
project and decided to use my MBA degree in finance to his advan-

tage. Gradually, the financial side of my job became more prominent, which later opened the door for the financial position I had desired all along. The Lord used my writing experience as the path to a position that resolved my financial dilemma.

4. Use Common Sense

Jonathan displayed common sense in his approach to the crisis posed by the Philistine army. While his plan at first appeared more than a little risky and far-fetched, we must again remember that he had grown up near the enemy garrison. I believe he knew exactly how to scale the cliff because he had done so earlier in his life. He used his familiarity with the precipice to formulate his plan of attack.

Jonathan also showed practical wisdom in determining the battle-readiness of the Philistines. He proposed a test to determine God's will that would reveal whether or not the enemy was prepared for the surprise attack he had in mind.

Saul, by way of contrast, was anything but practical in the orders he gave after the Lord's rout of the enemy began. First, the king delayed sending his troops into the battle while he vainly tried to determine the will of God. Second, he refused to allow the soldiers to eat, which limited their strength while they pursued the fleeing Philistines. Both commands displayed a blatant lack of common sense.

A mistake we often make is proceeding with a plan based on feelings rather than wisdom. "I prayed about God's will in this matter, and this is the way He is leading," we might say—even though the path might appear foolish at best.

I'm not at all saying we should never take a step of faith, but I often hear believers make reckless and hasty decisions based on emotions alone, which in the end makes situations worse, not better.

When we do take a step of faith, it's necessary to think things through and confirm what direction the Lord is truly leading us in.

Walking with God

What do the contrasting examples of Saul and Jonathan teach us about our walk with God? If our ultimate goal is to honor ourselves, we more times than not make unwise and hasty decisions. We remember the self-seeking Saul for his failures, not his successes.

Jonathan shows what we can accomplish when our ultimate desire is to see God glorified. He believed the Lord's promises about Israel and, against all odds, attacked the Philistines. God used Jonathan's plan to defeat His enemy.

Jonathan believed the fight was solely between God and the Philistines. He saw himself as merely a player in the drama, not the main attraction. He then acted with confidence in the Lord once he determined the Lord had led him to his decision. The Lord honored his faith.

Ronald Reagan once said, "There is no limit to the amount of good you can do if you don't care who gets the credit." While that's certainly true, Jonathan might have put it this way: "There is no limit to what you can do for God when you trust His promises and give Him all the glory for what He accomplishes through you."

STUDY GUIDE

Chapter 2

Saul: The King Who Cowered While His Son Climbed

Passage: 1 Samuel 14

Key verses: Psalm 139:17; Colossians 3:17

Questions for discussion:

1. Why do you think God honored Olympic athlete Eric Liddell's decision not to run on a Sunday?
2. How did Jonathan display his faith with his risky attack against the Philistines?
3. In what ways did Jonathan's strategy involve common sense?
4. Why do you think the Philistines panicked when Jonathan and his armor-bearer climbed the cliff and came against them?
5. In what ways did Saul bring attention to himself once he realized the Philistines were fleeing in panic?
6. Why was the king's prohibition on the Israelite soldiers eating so foolish?
7. What does it mean for you to have confidence in God's purposes?
8. How did Jonathan give glory to the Lord as he prepared to attack the Philistine outpost?
9. When might it be appropriate to use common sense and past experiences in making key decisions?

STUDY GUIDE

Chapter 2

10. What is your main take-away lesson from chapter 2?

Key lesson: If our objective is to honor ourselves with the choices we make, we more times than not make unwise decisions. We remember Saul for his failures and sins, not for his successes.

On the other hand, if we set our sights on honoring the Lord with the way we conduct ourselves and make decisions, He rewards our trust in Him. We remember Jonathan for his faith and humbleness.

3

JOAB

THE COMMANDER WHO MURDERED THOSE IN HIS WAY

What causes quarrels and what causes fights among you? Is it not
this, that your passions are at war within you? You desire and
do not have, so you murder. You covet and cannot obtain, so you
fight and quarrel. You do not have, because you do not ask.

—JAMES 4:1–2

After World War II, an insightful story came to light concerning the
German response to the Allies' invasion of Normandy on June 6,
1944. As you may remember from history lessons, weather conditions
over the English Channel were poor when General Dwight Eisenhower
gave the command to proceed with the assault. Although fog overshad-
owed the area, the forecast showed a chance for clearing, and Eisenhower based his decision on that prospect. The fate of Europe and the
lives of many brave soldiers rested on his shoulders. Would the weather
clear in time? Would the attack succeed?

Although they didn't know when or where, the Germans knew the invasion was coming and placed their top general, Erwin Rommel, in charge of defending France against the assault.

Because of the predicted fog over the English Channel on June 6, the Germans assumed the invasion wouldn't happen on that day. Taking advantage of the unanticipated break from the war, General Rommel decided to go home and surprise his wife for her birthday.

Further, thinking weather patterns precluded any attack from the Allied forces, Rommel's senior commanders scheduled a training exercise for June 6, which took them and their troops away from the command center as well.

By the time Rommel and his generals received word of the invasion and returned to their posts, it was too late to employ an effective counterstrategy to the invasion at Normandy.[4]

Do you see God's sovereign hand in what happened that day? He distracted the top German military leaders so they weren't ready to respond effectively to the invasion. On the other hand, God gave General Eisenhower confidence to go ahead with the attack despite poor weather conditions.

The Allied victory resulted from skilled leadership on the part of General Eisenhower as well as from the Lord's orchestration of events—including the weather and even the exact birthdate of Rommel's wife. God worked behind the scenes to ensure the Allies' success on the battlefield. We see this pattern throughout Scripture when God fought on behalf of the armies of Israel.

As the top commander of King David's forces, Joab led Israel to numerous triumphs through his God-given ability as a strategist. Joab, however, never grasped the full significance of the Lord's work for Israel. Despite watching God send panic-stricken armies into flight as they came against Joab, his faith remained in his head and never penetrated his heart.

One writer aptly summed up Joab's life this way:

This period of history was harsh and primitive, and Joab was a product of his age. He was a decisive, fearless, and intrepid fighter, and a brilliant military strategist. He served his king and his country devotedly. He was generous and loyal to his friends, but utterly ruthless and vindictive toward his foes. He was not completely devoid of religious sentiment, but it played no decisive part in his conduct. He died as he lived—by the sword.[5]

Hebrews 11:1 says: "Faith is the assurance of things hoped for, the conviction of things not seen." Verse 6 adds, "And without faith it is impossible to please [God], for whoever would draw near to God must believe that he exists and that he rewards those who seek him." Joab believed in the existence of God, but never possessed genuine, life-changing faith. He killed to preserve what he cherished, because his ultimate dream had to do with his position as leader of Israel's army rather than with his service to the Lord.

Brilliant Military Leader

Without a doubt, Joab was an outstanding field general. He won key battles for King David through his prowess as a superb strategist in the heat of battle. Joab spectacularly displayed these skills in the capture of Jerusalem. When David became king over all of Israel, the Jebusites controlled the city. Confident about their defenses and ability to defeat the new king, they sent this simple message to David: "You will not come in here" (1 Chronicles 11:5).

David, who already dearly loved Jerusalem, promised that whoever devised a strategy to successfully defeat the Jebusites would become the top commander of his army (1 Chronicles 11:6). Although Joab already served in that capacity, the king hoped someone else would step forward and claim the prized position. (David's motive will become clear at a later time.) However, Joab came up with the winning plan, led the Israelites to victory over the Jebusites, and retained his position as the leader of Israel's army.

We also see Joab's amazing skill as a military strategist in his defeat of an alliance consisting of the Ammonites and Syrians (2 Samuel 10). The incident began when David sent a few of his servants to console Hanun, the king of the Ammonites, whose father had recently died. Foolishly, Hanun regarded David's men as spies and treated them shamefully; he cut off their beards and a part of their clothing before sending them away (2 Samuel 10:1–5). Upon realizing David's furious response to the incident, Hanun hired thirty-three thousand Syrian soldiers to aid his war effort against Israel (2 Samuel 10:6).

As the battle began, Joab recognized his army was at a serious disadvantage because the enemy was attacking from both the front and rear. In the midst of the conflict, the commander devised a plan that turned what looked like a certain defeat into an astounding victory. He divided up his forces, putting his best soldiers against the Syrians and placing the others under the leadership of his brother Abishai to combat the inferior Ammonites (2 Samuel 10:7–11). This made good sense, because it matched Israel's best warriors against the Syrians, whose army was more than likely superior to that of the Ammonites.

Joab gave the following encouragement to his brother (his words were within earshot of the soldiers): "Be of good courage, and let us be courageous for our people, and for the cities of our God, and may the Lord do what seems good to him" (2 Samuel 10:12). With this statement, Joab wisely reminded his soldiers that they were fighting for their families back home, and he drew their attention to the Lord, who would fight for them.

Joab's daring scheme worked. Once he gained an advantage over the Syrians, they ran from the battle. When the Ammonites saw the Syrians' panic, they retreated in fear (2 Samuel 10:13–14). While Joab's plan displayed wisdom, it was, once again, the Lord who defeated the forces arrayed against the nation. As with Jonathan and his armor-bearer, God put fear into the hearts of the opposing armies, causing them to run from the battle.

If all we knew about Joab was the story of his triumph over the Ammonite and Syrian alliance, we might conclude that he was a man of great faith like other great military leaders of Israel such as Barak or Gideon (see Hebrews 11:32). Scripture, however, reveals a very dark side of Joab; he murdered to preserve what mattered to him the most.

Cold-Blooded Murderer

When David first became king, he ruled for seven years over the tribe of Judah while Ish-bosheth, a son of Saul, reigned over Israel's northern tribes. Abner, the capable military general under King Saul, remained loyal to Ish–bosheth. Early in the conflict between these two sides, Joab led David's army to victory against the forces loyal to the house of Saul.

In pursuing Abner after one of those battles, Joab's brother Asahel caught up to the opposing general and engaged him in a fight. Abner did not want to kill Asahel, but that proved to be the only way to stop his deadly pursuit (2 Samuel 2:12–23).

Joab never forgave Abner for killing his brother and later seized the opportunity to gain revenge.

Abner later grew weary of the continuing battles with David and decided to recognize the Lord's anointing on David as king over all Israel (2 Samuel 3:17–21). Abner went to David in peace, promising to help make him king over all the tribes of Israel.

Joab, however, became enraged when he heard the news and schemed to murder Abner. Under the pretense of having a special message for Abner, presumably from David, Joab took the unsuspecting man aside and murdered him (2 Samuel 3:26–27).

Joab had no just cause for revenge in this matter. Abner had killed his brother Asahel in the heat of battle and as an act of self-defense. Joab, on the other hand, had slain Abner under false premises during a

time of peace. It was nothing less than cold-hearted murder. (I believe it
was because of this slaying that David later hoped someone besides Joab
would capture Jerusalem and lead his army.)

I suspect Joab had an additional motivation for exacting his revenge.
Abner, as an experienced and capable military general, posed a significant threat to Joab's cherished position as the commander of the armies
under King David. As such, it's likely that Joab killed Abner not only as
an act of vengeance, but also to ensure that he would retain his position
as general. He feared the new alliance between David and Abner would
jeopardize his treasured role in the nation's leadership.

This motivation appears even more clearly in the second assassination committed by Joab. After David defeated the forces of Absalom,
another rebellion arose. Sheba, described as a "worthless man" from the
tribe of Benjamin, led this uprising. Sheba gathered soldiers from the
northern tribes to fight against David and the tribe of Judah. Rather
than ask Joab to put together an army in response to the uprising, David
assigned the task to Amasa (2 Samuel 20:1–4).

Why would David overlook Joab for leading his military? Earlier, in
defiance to the king's direct command, Joab had ordered his soldiers to
kill Absalom. Frustrated with his disobedience, David once again looked
for someone else to lead his armies, one who would obey his orders.
Joab, as you might expect, did not take kindly to the snubbing.

Recognizing the threat, Joab murdered Amasa. While purporting to
be concerned with Amasa's welfare, he took him aside and killed him with
a concealed sword (2 Samuel 20:8–10). The motive was purely personal.
Amasa posed a new obstacle to Joab's role of continuing to lead the armies
of Israel. He stood in the way of what Joab wanted the most in this life.

Solomon Administers Overdue Justice

Although David didn't take immediate action against Joab, he noted
Joab's evil behavior and later ensured that he would pay for his wicked

behavior. In his final instructions to Solomon, David asked his son to administer the overdue justice. First Kings 2:5–6 says:

> Moreover, you also know what Joab the son of Zeruiah did to me, how he dealt with the two commanders of the armies of Israel, Abner the son of Ner, and Amasa the son of Jether, whom he killed, avenging in time of peace for blood that had been shed in war, and putting the blood of war on the belt around his waist and on the sandals on his feet. Act therefore according to your wisdom, but do not let his gray head go down to Sheol in peace.

David recognized Joab's treachery. He had killed in times of peace, using deception to conceal his deadly intent. Why didn't David deal with Joab himself rather than leave it to Solomon? Some commentators suggest it was because of Joab's fierce loyalty to the king. Others say it was because David involved Joab in the killing of Uriah after the king's encounter with Bathsheba (see 2 Samuel 11:14-27) and perhaps feared more repercussions from that.

Solomon, on the other hand, had his own reason for administering justice to Joab. In the last weeks of David's life, another one of David's sons, Adonijah, declared himself king. Joab unwisely supported this coup in defiance of David's wishes about who would succeed him. David responded to the rebellion by installing Solomon as the king of Israel, the one he had intended all along to take his place (1 Kings 1:9–40).

Fearing revenge for his support of Solomon's brother, Joab fled to the tabernacle and grabbed hold of the horns of the altar. He may have thought this final appeal to God would save him from justice. It didn't. King Solomon instructed Benaiah, who would replace Joab as the commander of Israel's army, to kill him despite his position near the Temple (1 Kings 2:28–35).

His final plea for God's intervention fits with all we've seen throughout the rest of his life. When he felt a need for the Lord, he held on to his knowledge of the Law, hoping that would spare him from death.

This last act of seeking God, just like all his other attempts at worship, was superficial at best.

Signs of Superficial Faith

Even genuine followers of Jesus can fall victim to a superficial faith such as we see in the example of Joab.

James, the brother of Jesus, addressed this issue in the book he wrote to early believers. "What good is it, my brothers," he asked, "if someone says he has faith but does not have works? Can that faith save him?" (James 2:14). James is not contradicting the Apostle Paul, who proclaimed that God saves us entirely by grace alone through faith (Ephesians 2:8–9). James simply points out the danger of possessing a lifeless faith that does not change one's heart or impact a person's life in any way.

Joab was just such a poser. He could talk the part, but his faith never touched his heart.

What are the signs of a superficial faith that remains in one's head and does not regenerate the heart?

1. It Settles for Pious-Sounding Words That Don't Reflect a Changed Heart.

When Charles Colson was still alive, I received daily emails from his BreakPoint ministry. I enjoyed reading his comments on current events; he provided wise insights into the headlines of the day and cultural trends. In one of his emails, Colson told the story of a woman who went to her pastor seeking counsel regarding her physically abusive husband, who happened to be an elder at the church. Perhaps because the man was a leader, the pastor instructed the woman to submit to her husband and trust the Lord to work on his heart.

The woman's story ended tragically. Not long after her visit with the pastor, she died at the hands of her husband. While the man's spiritual-sounding words had convinced the church, as well as his pastor, of his fitness for godly leadership, they simply masked the anger raging inside him. Doesn't this sound like Joab, who at times talked like a man of great faith, while at other times killed those in his way?

Colson's story is an extreme example, yet we all feel the pull to sound pious, to use religious jargon that doesn't match the reality inside us. We settle for sounding spiritual even though we know our speech doesn't reflect our true devotion to the Savior.

Joab lived under the Law, and while he might have complied with many of its external demands, he did so without recognizing its implications for his heart. Satan loves to convince believers that faith consists of outward adherence to a set of rules or morals. If Satan can keep them from walking in the life-changing power of the Holy Spirit, he can lock them into a superficial faith. This, of course, renders them ineffective in using their gifts to serve God.

Joab's example teaches us the folly of depending on religious appearance (speech and behavior) rather than seeking the renewed heart that only comes through saving faith in Jesus (Titus 3:4–7). We can never change ourselves from the outside in. Only God can change us—and He does it from the inside out.

Joab's story also warns us about how people can deceive those around them. Some folks may initially seem charming, spiritual, and congenial. It's only after we wrong them or find ourselves in a close relationship with them that their genuine hateful and vengeful spirit emerges. Solomon wrote about this in Proverbs 26:23–27 cautioning us against people who speak "graciously" but harbor "deceit" and "hatred" inside their hearts.

2. It Attacks Those in Its Way.

James 4 adds this warning: "What causes quarrels and what causes fights among you? Is it not this, that your passions are at war within you? You desire and do not have, so you murder. You covet and cannot obtain, so you fight and quarrel. You do not have, because you do not ask" (vv. 1–2). Doesn't this sound a lot like Joab?

When he saw that someone stood in the way of his prized aspiration, leading the armies of Israel, he murdered him. Joab, however, never even bothered to quarrel; he just killed the one he saw as an obstacle to getting what he wanted.

Like the readers James addressed in his letter, Joab did not bother to ask the Lord to fulfill his desire and then trust Him with his life. He simply took matters into his own hands.

Was cold-blooded murder a problem among the readers of James' epistle? Most likely not; most commentators believe these early believers used other means to harm their fellow saints. It's far more probable that they used words or other nonlethal means to inflict pain on those who stood in the way of what they desired.

In the book of Proverbs, Solomon often referred to the harm our words can cause to others. I like this proverb in particular: "There is one whose rash words are like sword thrusts, but the tongue of the wise brings healing" (Proverbs 12:18). Our tongues can be just as hurtful and deadly as Joab's sword thrusts into the bellies of his adversaries.

Our words have the capacity to maim, kill, and destroy others.

In the Sermon on the Mount, Jesus said hateful words spoken in anger against others make us guilty of breaking the commandment forbidding murder (Matthew 5:21–22). This must have shocked those listening to Him that day. They were undoubtedly confident they could at least keep that commandment. But no, Jesus raised the standard higher than anyone could have imagined. They could commit murder with mean-spirited words directed in anger toward others. Now no one could say they kept that commandment!

Attacking those who get in our way is a behavior much more prevalent among believers than we care to admit. Take marriage, for example. We see our spouse standing in the way of our happiness and an argument erupts. *How dare he or she interfere with what I want?* Soon, harsh words ensue and cause lasting pain. This also happens when we use hurtful language with our children, blare the horn at slow drivers, or speak rudely to coworkers. Sadly, I have done all of these things and later begged for forgiveness.

The Apostle Paul warned: "Let no corrupting talk come out of your mouths, but only such as is good for building up, as fits the occasion, that it may give grace to those who hear" (Ephesians 4:29). Rather than harm others with our speech, the Lord wants us to encourage others in their walk of faith and exhibit a spirit of grace rather than of condemnation.

Walking with God

What does Joab teach us about our walk with God? We must depend on Him for the desires of our heart rather than attack those we believe stand in our way. In other words, we need to trust God's character as a kind and loving Father—even when He says "no" to our prayers or when we never obtain what we long for the most.

It means we believe the Lord has our best interests at heart for all He allows into our lives. Jesus said, "These things I have spoken to you, that my joy may be in you, and that your joy may be full" (John 15:11). The Lord doesn't come into our hearts to thwart our happiness and steal our joy. He loves us dearly and has our ultimate best interests at heart—for now and for eternity.

Paul wrote this in Romans 8:32: "He who did not spare his own Son but gave him up for us all, how will he not also with him graciously give us all things?" If we believe what the apostle says, we can relax rather than attack those we view as blocking the path to what we want. *The Lord may be allowing that person to divert us to a better path.*

We may never understand the reasons for all we endure, but in eternity we will see the full picture and recognize how all the paths God led us down fit with His eternal plans for us.

We will reign with Jesus during the Millennium and then forever in the eternal state. Could the Lord be preparing us now for our future roles through the pain and troubles He lets come our way before that time? I'm convinced He's doing exactly that. He's getting us ready to fulfill our purpose in His Kingdom. How exciting is that?!

The story of our lives as New Testament saints extends into eternity; it does not end at our death or with the Rapture. The Lord's never-ending goodness will continue far beyond what we can see or even imagine!

The best news of all is that no one can cancel our joyous hope!

STUDY GUIDE
Chapter 3

Joab: The Commander Who Murdered Those in His Way

Passages: 2 Samuel 3:26–30; 10:1–19; 20:1–10
Key verses: James 4:1–4; Proverbs 12:18; Romans 8:32

Questions for discussion:

1. What examples do we see in Scripture of Joab's superior ability as a military leader and strategist?
2. What other motive, besides revenge, did Joab have for murdering Abner?
3. Why did Joab kill Amasa?
4. Why do you suppose David hesitated to punish Joab?
5. In what way was Joab a poser, someone who could talk the talk, but never lived by trusting in the Lord?
6. How do the warnings of James 4:1–4 apply to Joab? To us?
7. What ways do believers have of striking back at those who get in their way (assuming murder is not an option)?
8. Can you think of a time in your past when you may have attempted to remove or injure a person who stood in the way of getting what you wanted?
9. How does the eternal nature of your walk with the Lord enable you to stay closer to Him during sad and painful times?

STUDY GUIDE

Chapter 3

Key lesson: Walking with God means we depend on Him for the fulfillment of our desires rather than attack other people we believe are standing in our way. A mature faith doesn't lash out at those we suppose are hindering us from what we desire; it leaves the outcome solely in the hands of the Lord.

4

ABSALOM

THE HANDSOME PRINCE WHO BECAME A TICKING TIME BOMB

*Anger and bitterness are two noticeable signs of being focused
on self and not trusting God's sovereignty in your life. When
you believe that God causes all things to work together for good
to those who belong to Him and love Him, you can respond to
trials with joy instead of anger or bitterness.*

—John C. Broger

For forty-three years, a Ukrainian woman, Zinaida Bragantsova,
had been telling people a World War II bomb was buried under
her bed.

The Associated Press published a report about it several years ago:

The story began in 1941 when the Germans advanced toward
the Ukrainian city of Berdyansk. One night at the very start of
the war, she was sitting by the window and sewing on her machine. Suddenly a noise was heard and a whistling close by. She
got up and in the following moment was struck by a blast of

wind. When she came to, the sewing machine was gone and there was a hole in the floor as well as in the ceiling.

Zinaida couldn't get any officials to check out her story, so she just moved her bed over the hole and lived with it for the next 40 years. Finally, the woman's problem was uncovered. As phone cable was being laid in the area, demolition experts were called in to probe for buried explosives. "Where's your bomb, grandma?" asked the smiling army lieutenant sent to talk to Mrs. Bragantsova. "No doubt, under your bed?"

"Under my bed," Mrs. Bragantsova answered dryly.

"And sure enough, there they found a 500–pound bomb. After evacuating 2,000 people from surrounding buildings, the bomb squad detonated the bomb. According to the report, "The grandmother, freed of her bomb, will soon receive a new apartment."[6]

This unfortunate woman had lived with a bomb beneath her bed for decades because no one believed her story. During all that time, no one in Zinaida's neighborhood was entirely safe until the authorities located the bomb and removed or disarmed it. Until then, it had the potential to cause great harm.

Scripture describes bitterness in the same way.

The writer of Hebrews gives us this warning: "See to it that no one fails to obtain the grace of God; that no 'root of bitterness' springs up and causes trouble, and by it many become defiled" (Hebrews 12:15). Resentment stems from a poisonous root that stirs up trouble in one's own soul, and it soon affects others with its deadly toxins.

We see this in the life of Absalom. Once bitterness took control of his heart, he became a danger to himself and those around him. Like a ticking time bomb, the animosity inside him grew until it exploded. By the end of his life, twenty thousand Israeli soldiers had died as a result of the bitter spirit he nurtured over the course of many years.

But I'm getting ahead of the story.

Tragedy Sparks Bitterness

Absalom's bitterness stemmed from one of the more sordid stories in all of Scripture. His angry response to this tragic event opened the door for the foul spirit of resentment to gain control of his soul.

Absalom had a sister named Tamar, a beautiful and godly young woman whose great beauty unfortunately attracted the attention of Amnon, her half-brother. With the help of a cousin named Jonadab, Amnon devised a plot so he could be alone with Tamar (2 Samuel 13:1–5). The initial step involved Ammon pretending to be sick.

The plan worked. David went to check on his supposedly ill son and, in response to Amnon's request, the king asked Tamar to cook some cakes in the presence of her half-brother. Once she finished her task, Amnon ordered everyone present to leave. Then he raped Tamar. After that, he put her outside his door; he no longer wished to have anything to do with her (2 Samuel 13:6–14).

Absalom took his devastated and shamed sister into his house and sought to comfort her. Absalom loved Tamar dearly; he later named one of his daughters after her (2 Samuel 14:27). While the text at this point doesn't specifically tell of Absalom's growing anger over this tragic incident, it clearly fumed inside him. He refused to even talk to Amnon, but such was just the beginning of his hostility toward him (2 Samuel 13: 22).

The Bible says David was "very angry" when he heard what Amnon had done, but he did nothing in response (2 Samuel 13:21). Some believe David's own sin with Bathsheba kept him from punishing his son. It's also possible he felt partly responsible because of his role in asking Tamar to cook for Amnon.

Absalom waited two years before taking matters into his own hands, perhaps delaying his response because he was waiting for his father to do something. David, however, never punished Amnon for his wicked act, nor do we read of the king even admonishing his evil son.

Besides his displeasure at his father's inaction, another factor may have added to Absalom's growing resentment. Amnon, David's oldest son, was the heir apparent to the throne at the time. He may have asked himself, "How could my father keep Amnon in line to be king after what he has done? Don't I deserve to be the next king of Israel?" As these questions, along with his sister's suffering, plagued him, his thoughts turned murderous.

Two years later, Absalom staged a party for all his brothers. His purpose for the gathering, however, was to kill Amnon. Absalom ordered his servants to kill Amnon after he had become drunk with wine. He knew his brother well enough to know he could count on him to become intoxicated, thus providing the opportunity for his assassination. Absalom told his servants not to fear; he would take full responsibility for their deed (2 Samuel 13:23–29).

Absalom had valid reasons to be angry, but killing Amnon did not solve anything. It certainly didn't stem his growing fury. His rage only intensified as the rift between him and his father widened during the following years.

Explosion!

Fearing how his father might respond to the murder of Amnon, Absalom fled to nearby Geshur, where a man named Talmai reigned as king (2 Samuel 13:34–39). Geshur was a small kingdom located within the modern nation of Syria. King Talmai was Absalom's maternal grandfather (2 Samuel 3:3), whom Absalom believed would protect him.

Absalom's flight from Israel was, in all likelihood, unnecessary. In 2 Samuel 13:37, we read that after Absalom ran away, "David mourned for his son day after day." While some believe this is a reference to Amnon, it's more likely that David was grieving for Absalom. Verse 39 adds that the king's spirit "longed to go out to Absalom, because he was comforted about Amnon, since he was dead." David may also have been afraid of how it would look if he welcomed Absalom back after he had murdered his brother. As a result, David and Absalom remained apart as the bitterness inside the son grew and grew.

Second Samuel 14 records the ruse Joab used to convince King David to allow his son to return to Jerusalem. Although David recognized Joab's role behind the ploy, he nevertheless allowed Joab to bring Absalom back to Israel. According to the king's instructions, Absalom would not live in the palace (2 Samuel 14:21–24). Such an arrangement, which cut him off from royal life and his father's presence, did little to appease the son's growing sense of entitlement to the throne.

In the midst of the drama of Absalom's return, the writer of 2 Samuel added this intriguing note: "Now in all Israel there was no one so much to be praised for his handsome appearance as Absalom. From the sole of his foot to the crown of his head there was no blemish in him" (2 Samuel 14:25). Undoubtedly, his good looks and popularity increased Absolom's sense of entitlement; it certainly contributed to his ability to influence the people of Israel.

Absalom was the third-oldest son of the king. Amnon, the firstborn, was now dead, and, since Scripture tells us nothing about the second in line, Chileab, apart from his birth, it's likely he wasn't a significant factor. Who else would be the next king?

Absalom might have thought his return to Jerusalem would place him in good standing with his father again, but such was not the case. In order to obtain the throne he believed rightfully belonged to him, Absalom soon realized he needed to take action to at least gain access to his father. In desperation, he set fire to one of Joab's fields to seek his attention. It worked. Joab soon thereafter facilitated a meeting between David and his son, which resulted in Absalom having greater access to the palace (2 Samuel 14:28–33).

Absalom, however, wanted more than that; he wanted to be the king. He soon formed a plan to use his new privileges to undermine David's leadership and thereby hasten his own rise to power.

Absalom appealed to the people as someone who would be a more compassionate judge than his father. In those days, the role of the king included presiding as judge over difficult legal cases in the nation. Absalom cleverly convinced many of the people he could do a better job as their judge; he promised to give them the justice they deserved (2 Samuel 15:1–6). He was a masterful politician.

After he had obtained a significant following, Absalom put a plot in motion to take the throne by force. The bitterness festering within him had now exploded. On a trip to Hebron to purportedly "worship the Lord," Absalom gathered enough of a following to force David to leave Jerusalem and flee for his life (2 Samuel 15:7–17).

Tragic End

(Spoiler alert!) The story did not end well for Absalom. Second Samuel 17–18 provides the grim details of his defeat and death.

The silence of Scripture regarding the faith of Absalom speaks volumes. At no point do we see him seeking or acknowledging the Lord in any way. His life consisted of pursuing what he wanted, regardless of the consequences. As his resentment toward his dad grew, it's safe to assume his anger intensified toward the Lord as well.

Isn't this often the case for us also? Harboring an unforgiving attitude toward others more often than not leads to blaming God for our predicament. I've seen this tendency many times in others as well as in myself. Bitterness toward another person eventually broadens to include the Lord in the scope of its anger; *it always happens that way*.

Once in Jerusalem, Absalom received advice from both Ahithophel and Hushai. Not aware that Hushai remained loyal to David, Absalom accepted his advice and rejected the path laid out by Ahithophel. Second Samuel 17:14 tells us God intended to "bring harm upon Absalom." As a result, the Lord caused Absalom to choose Hushai's advice, which delayed a conflict with his father and spared David's life.

Rather than strike immediately as Ahithophel proposed, Absalom waited to gather a larger fighting force, then went into battle himself

(2 Samuel 17:25–18:5). This proved to be fatal as his father's army readily defeated that of Absalom and his followers. Unfortunately, twenty thousand soldiers lost their lives during the conflict between Absalom and his dad (2 Samuel 18:7). The ticking time bomb of Absalom's bitterness exploded with fatal consequences for a great many in Israel.

As Absalom fled from the battle scene, his head—or, more likely, his long hair—became entangled in the branches of a tree (2 Samuel 18:9–10). Joab discovered the king's son hanging helplessly from the tree and commanded his men to kill him (2 Samuel 18:11–15). Even though David had previously commanded Joab to spare Absalom's life, he knew the only way to finally end the revolt was to kill him.

Uprooting Bitterness

My purpose for focusing on the Bible's bad guys isn't merely to increase your biblical knowledge, but to enable all of us to learn from their mistakes. From Absalom's life, we see the necessity of uprooting bitterness before it produces its deadly fruit, destroys close relationships, damages churches, leads us away from the Lord, and potentially ruins the lives of those around us.

Hebrews 12:15 compares bitterness to a poisonous root: Once it takes hold of the soul, it spreads throughout the rest of our life. Unless it's uprooted and replaced with forgiveness and grace, the toxins sour our thoughts and attitudes, especially about those we deem responsible for our pain.

Such was the case with my Uncle Albert. When I think of a bitter person, he immediately comes to mind. He continually complained that his brothers had cheated him out of his share of his parents' inheritance and over time he became consumed with resentment that continued until the day he died. I sometimes wonder if his multiple surgeries for ulcers and other related stomach ailments resulted from the fury that raged inside him.

Let's look at four steps we can take to prevent a spirit of resentment from wreaking havoc within us.

1. Quickly Resolve Anger

The best way to keep bitter feelings from taking root is to deal quickly with the anger that caused them. In Ephesians 4:26–27, Paul says, "Be angry and do not sin; do not let the sun go down on your anger, and give no opportunity to the devil."

The apostle doesn't say our angry feelings themselves constitute sin, but when we nurture our anger, we give the devil a foothold for damaging us and others. That's why he instructs us to resolve our feelings of anger as quickly as possible before they spill over into sin.

A story from the early days of baseball illustrates how much damage anger can do. During the 1894 baseball season, the Baltimore Orioles traveled to Boston to play a regular-season game. During the contest, the Oriole's John McGraw and Boston's third baseman got into a fight. Players from both benches soon joined the brawl, which spilled from the field to the stands. During the fight, someone set fire to the grandstands and the ballpark burned to the ground. The fire soon spread to buildings in the nearby neighborhood, damaging more than one hundred structures in Boston.

In the course of our lives, others will wrong us; we can count on that. We might also read about grave injustices in the world and feel a surge of anger. This happens often in these perilous times. However, even if we can justify our anger based on the wicked behavior of others or our news feeds, we must not let it fester and turn into bitterness.

When we refuse to deal with anger in a timely manner, Satan seizes the opportunity to stir up trouble inside us, just as Paul warned in Ephesians 4:26–27. When that happens, Satan's agents, which we refer to as "demons," establish a stronghold in our lives wherein they cultivate bitterness, with its harmful and tragic impact on us and others.

2. Put on Humility Rather Than Pride

Absalom's temptation to be proud was perhaps far greater than anything we will ever encounter. He was the third-oldest son of King David and grew up enjoying privileges few in his day could imagine. He was also exceedingly handsome and had beautiful long hair; everyone in Israel praised him because of his appearance (2 Samuel 14:25–26). If he were alive today, he would no doubt win *People* magazine's award for being the "sexiest man alive."

Such overwhelming admiration no doubt strengthened Absalom's sense of entitlement to the throne, among other things, and his endearing charm enabled him to influence many people.

In Absalom's day, dignitaries emphasized their regal importance by riding mules. His decision to ride a mule into battle against his father was an arrogant decision on Absalom's part (although he would have had a much better chance of escaping from the battle alive if he had been riding a horse).

What might have happened if, before he murdered Amnon, Absalom had humbly bowed before the Lord and asked Him to work out the matter according to His purposes? What if Absalom had approached his father with an unassuming spirit and asked him to deal with Amnon's sin? We don't know how either of these scenarios might have changed the outcome, but it's likely the story would have ended far better for Absalom.

Because of David's great love for Absalom, I believe Absalom might have become king after David's death had he dealt differently with his sister's tragedy. Yes, his father should have administered justice, but Absalom's immense pride and unforgiving spirit led to bitter inner turmoil, which later led to his death.

3. Forgive Others!

Jesus' parable in Matthew 18:23–35 has often helped me forgive others instead of holding a grudge. In the account, a king graciously forgives a man's enormous debt after listening to his pleas for mercy. The monarch's mercy kept him, his wife, and children from a life of slavery to repay the huge obligation. Later, the one absolved of the great burden refuses to extend the same grace to another person who couldn't repay an amount that was only a small fraction of what the king had already forgiven him.

I often imagine the Lord's forgiveness of my sins as being worth hundreds of millions of dollars or much more, while I value the sins of those committed against me at anywhere from one hundred to a thousand dollars. As I reflect on the seriousness of my sins, which the Lord has already so graciously forgiven, it helps me to let go of far smaller offenses. Whenever I sense an unforgiving spirit arising, I use Jesus' parable to resolve my unwillingness to release the offenses committed against me. I sometimes need to repeat this many times.

While wrongs against us may be substantial and painful, they pale in comparison to our sins against our heavenly Father. Since God has completely forgiven all our many sins (those in the past, the present, and the future), how can we refuse to forgive others? This perspective has often helped me let go of anger toward others who have hurt me.

I've also found that, once I forgive someone, I need to be on guard against feelings of anger or bitterness that begin to creep back into my soul, especially if the offenders have never apologized or even realized they offended me. My desire is to remove all bitterness from my heart, but at times I have to repeatedly remind myself that God is able to work all things for my "good" (Romans 8:28).

Like Joseph, I tell myself that, although others may have "meant evil against me, God meant it for good" (Genesis 50:20).

4. Recognize the Fatal Outcome of Bitterness

Someone once said, "Unforgiveness is like drinking poison and hoping the other person dies."[7] A merciless attitude works like that. We easily deceive ourselves into thinking the object of our anger will suffer, but in reality, bitterness damages us far more than it does the person who harmed us. As Absalom fumed over what Amnon had done to his sister, he couldn't foresee how his rage would destroy *himself.* He certainly didn't picture himself hanging from a tree watching Joab's soldiers throw spears at him.

Life rarely—no, never—turns out well for people consumed by bitterness. Absalom is just one glaring example of the ultimate outcome for those who live in such a way. A few years ago, a man from Illinois became embittered by the political climate in America and shot at a group of Republican congressmen practicing for their annual charity baseball game. After he severely wounded a prominent legislator, the police fired back and killed the gunman. Similar to Absalom, that man's bitterness and hatred blinded him to reality and led to his violent death.

It may not seem like the most pious of motives, but simply recognizing the harmful consequences of our resentment and unforgiving spirit can help us choose the path the apostle laid out in Ephesians 4:26–27—that of quickly dealing with our feelings of anger. The bitter people I've known have become factors in my desire to avoid turning out like them.

Life quickly taught me, however, that it takes much more than a natural inclination to avoid bitterness. It requires dependence on the Holy Spirit along with a firm, ongoing dependence on Scripture. A desire to avoid bitterness is not enough when others brutally attack us or dismiss our feelings.

The book of Proverbs often speaks of the contrasting outcomes of righteous living versus wicked behavior. Proverbs 14:12 says, "There is a way that seems right to a man, but its end is the way to death." I'm sure Absalom believed his actions were just, yet, in the end, he found himself warring against God—and that never turns out in one's favor.

Walking with God

What does Absalom's example teach us about our walk with God? It demonstrates our need to bring the truths of the Gospel into the wounds inflicted on us by others.

There are times when we feel devalued, rejected, or insulted by what others say about us or do to us; these things surely happen. Rather than respond in anger or allow bitterness to boil up, we must submit the matter to the Lord and remember what He has done through His death on the cross and Resurrection.

Looking at life through the lens of the Gospel allows us to see that the Lord has treated us far more graciously and mercifully than we deserve. Jesus' righteousness belongs to us; God has already imputed it to us (2 Corinthians 5:21). How could we imagine we're even remotely worthy of that? Yet the Lord in His great mercy has granted us righteous standing before our Father in Heaven. Ephesians 1:4 says we are "holy and blameless" before the Lord. And so we are! It's all of grace!

The Lord forgives all the sins of those who believe in Him; He adopts them into His family and gives them eternal life, which we can never lose or forfeit. He gives us a brand-new identity at the moment He saves us that no one can take away.

Jesus' parable in Matthew 18:23–35 gives us much-needed perspective for everyday life. Living as people who've been forgiven a great debt that we could never repay radically changes our perspective when others wrong us, or when we hear or read about the grievous wickedness of others.

When we underestimate our own dire need for forgiveness, we often fail to extend mercy to others who wrong or injure us.

An unforgiving and bitter spirit springs from not understanding the seriousness of our sins toward God versus those committed against us. If we find ourselves unwilling to forgive the others' offenses, it signifies that we don't have a true grasp of the gravity of our sins against our Lord that He has freely and graciously forgiven.

It's critical that we never forget our Gospel-driven identity *when*, not *if*, others harm us.

STUDY GUIDE

Chapter 4

that we don't have a full grasp of the gravity of our sins against our Lord

that He has freely and graciously forgiven.

Perhaps that means we need to spend more time identifying how our sin affects others (harms us).

Absalon:
The Handsome Prince Who Became a Ticking Time Bomb

Passage: 2 Samuel 13–18
Key verses: Hebrews 12:15; Ephesians 4:26–27; Matthew 18:23–35

Questions for discussion:

1. How did the tragic incident of Ammon and Tamar affect Absalom?
2. How might his dad's lack of response to Ammon's wickedness have contributed to Absalom's growing bitterness?
3. Do you think Absalom really needed to flee after killing Ammon?
4. How did Absalom work to gain the favor of the people?
5. What factors led to Absalom's sense of entitlement?
6. Why is it so important to quickly resolve feelings of anger? What happens when we don't?
7. What does Matthew 18:23–35 teach us about the importance of forgiving others? How does the comparison Jesus gave in this passage relate to our story?
8. How does looking at life through the lens of the Gospel enable us to forgive others?

STUDY GUIDE
Chapter 4

9. In what ways do you underestimate your own sins in comparison with those around you?
10. After reading this chapter, what comes to your mind when you think of Absalom, and how does that help you in your walk with the Lord?

Key lesson: Absalom teaches us the necessity of not letting anger grow inside us until it becomes bitterness. So often, when that happens, it explodes—hurting not only us, but those around us. Understanding the Gospel and its message of forgiveness enables us to deal with anger before it reaches that point.

5

AHITHOPHEL

THE KING'S ADVISOR WHO SOUGHT REVENGE

Repay no one evil for evil, but give thought to do what is honorable in the sight of all. If possible, so far as it depends on you, live peaceably with all. Beloved, never avenge yourselves, but leave it to the wrath of God, for it is written, "Vengeance is mine, I will repay, says the Lord."

—ROMANS 12:17–19

A s the movie ended, I felt a pang of guilt. I was watching the 2002 release of *The Count of Monte Cristo*, a story set in France during the time of Napoleon Bonaparte. The hero of the film, Edmond Dantés, had become caught up in the political intrigue of the day, only later to have his close friend, Fernand Mondego, betray him.

As a result of Mondego's treachery and the actions of a corrupt magistrate, Edmond ended up in a horrific island prison. Isolated in his cell, his only contact with others consisted of the prison guard, who routinely beat him, especially at first. Back in France, Fernand convinced

Edmond's fiancé that her lover was dead; he soon married her, which had been his motive for betraying his friend.

After six years of languishing in prison, Edmond's bleak outlook changed when a fellow prisoner, Abbé Faria, dug his way into Edmond's cell. He told Edmond about the location of an immense treasure—a prospect that motivated them to work on an escape tunnel. When Abbé died before they had completed the work, Edmond switched places with him by sewing himself into Abbé's body bag, which the prison guard later threw into the sea.

Years after his escape, Edmond used the map given to him by Abbé Faria and found the treasure, which made him enormously wealthy. He changed his name to "the Count of Monte Cristo," a title fitting the vastness of his riches, and began plotting revenge against his former friend.

As I became increasingly immersed in the plot, I found myself cheering on Edmond's plan. Why shouldn't he exact justice on the one who betrayed him? As his plot unfolded, I felt ashamed of my support for Edmond's vengeful agenda. As Edmond prevailed over Fernand in the end, he also felt the vanity of his revenge. He then vowed to use his vast wealth for good instead of seeking further retribution against his former enemies.

As we examine the life of Ahithophel, a once-trusted confidant and adviser to King David, we see a remarkable similarity to Edmond. He wanted revenge against someone who had once been a close friend and, as a result, joined Absalom's treacherous revolt against the king he had once loved and served.

The Motive

What caused Ahithophel to eagerly jump into Absalom's insurrection? The only motive that sufficiently explains his drastic change of heart toward David comes from his close ties to Bathsheba and her husband, Uriah. They were family. Second Samuel 11:3 identifies Bathsheba as "the daughter of Eliam." Later in 2 Samuel, we read that Eliam was "the son of Ahithophel the Gilonite" (2 Samuel 23:34). So, Ahithophel was the grandfather of Bathsheba and apparently had strong affections for both her and Uriah.

God's Word doesn't spell out Ahithophel's exact thoughts regarding David's affair with Bathsheba and the subsequent killing of Uriah. However, we do read about his willingness to join Absalom's revolt against the king. What other cause could there be for such a dramatic change in his attitude toward the king? What else would make this once-close confidant of David so eager to kill him?

It appears that Ahithophel did not accept the genuineness of David's repentance, or perhaps he believed the Lord had been far too lenient with him, given the nature of his offense. The Law prescribed death as the penalty in such cases. "Why does the Lord allow David to continue as king?" Ahithophel may have asked himself and others around him.

Once Absalom began his revolt, he sent for Ahithophel (2 Samuel 15:12). Why did Absalom think one of David's closest advisers would so eagerly betray him? He had heard of Ahithophel's disgust with the king and already knew of his willingness to join the coup.

The text simply says Absalom sent for him. He didn't need to explain what was happening; Ahithophel expected the king's son to summon him so he could help with the insurrection. All he needed was notification that it had started.

The Betrayal

Once in Jerusalem, Ahithophel counseled Absalom, saying, "Go in to your father's concubines, whom he has left to keep the house, and all Israel will hear that you have made yourself a stench to your father, and the hands of all who are with you will be strengthened" (2 Samuel 16:21). Why would this beloved counselor of David tell Absalom to exhibit such wicked behavior?

Some commentators suggest Ahithophel prescribed this course of action to protect himself. Now that he had joined forces with Absalom, his fate rested on the success of the revolt. The highly offensive nature of Absalom's conduct here would eliminate any chance of reconciliation between him and David. Ahithophel knew if Absalom and David ever reunited, the king would kill him for his treachery, while Absalom, whom David dearly loved, would likely escape such punishment.

Not only do we see self-interest in Ahithophel's advice, but in it we also see his deep hatred for David. It didn't matter that Absalom would be committing a great sin; Ahithophel wanted revenge. Disgracing David's concubines was just the first step.

Second Samuel 17:1–4 provides more of the counselors' guidance:

> Ahithophel said to Absalom, "Let me choose twelve thousand men, and I will arise and pursue David tonight. I will come upon him while he is weary and discouraged and throw him into a panic, and all the people who are with him will flee. I will strike down only the king, and I will bring all the people back to you as a bride comes home to her husband. You seek the life of only one man, and all the people will be at peace." And the advice seemed right in the eyes of Absalom and all the elders of Israel.

The plan was wise, bold, and likely to succeed, since David would be weary from his rapid departure from Jerusalem and not yet ready to defend himself.

With Ahithophel's proposal, Absalom would stay in the safety of the capital while Ahithophel led the army against David. It's noteworthy that Ahithophel wanted not only to lead the fight, but also to be the one to plunge his sword into David. This confirms the depth of his hatred as well as how personal it had become; he wanted to kill the king himself. This has all the earmarks of someone out for vengeance.

Although the plan sounded good to Absalom, he asked to also hear the counsel of another close adviser of David, Hushai the Archite. After initially fleeing with the king, Hushai returned to Jerusalem pretending to join the revolt (2 Samuel 15:32–37). David sent Hushai back to steer Absalom away from the advice of Ahithophel, whom he knew would provide Absalom with expert guidance.

Hushai persuaded Absalom to wait until all of Israel had gathered to him and then lead a larger army out to overtake David. If he suffered a defeat too early with too few soldiers, Hushai reasoned, those with him might lose heart at the prospect of again going up against his father. If that happened, he might forgo any chance of success (2 Samuel 17:5–13).

The delay sounded good to the king's son, and he chose the advice of Hushai over that of Ahithophel. Absalom might have thought he was making the choice himself, but Scripture says "the Lord had ordained" that he would choose the advice of Hushai (2 Samuel 17:14).

Hushai then sent word to David warning him of the possibility of an imminent attack. He may have feared Absalom would revert to Ahithophel's wiser plan (2 Samuel 17:15–26). To make sure he was safe against an ambush, the tired king moved farther away from Jerusalem.

Suicide

When Ahithophel saw that Absalom had spurned his advice, he traveled back to his home. It's likely no one had ever rejected his expert counsel. In addition to the shame he felt at this rejection of his guidance, he knew his plan was far superior and would have succeeded. Ahithophel recognized that God was still with David, and he knew the revolt would end in disaster.

Ahithophel "set his house in order and hanged himself, and he died and was buried in the tomb of his father" (2 Samuel 17:23). He decided to end his life on his own terms rather than wait for the uprising to fail, which would have resulted in his shameful and public execution. He wanted to avoid such a disgraceful end to his illustrious career.

Regarding Ahithophel's advice, Scripture says, "Now in those days the counsel that Ahithophel gave was as if one consulted the word of God; so was all the counsel of Ahithophel esteemed, both by David and by Absalom" (2 Samuel 16:23). He had an impeccable record of providing wise counsel. It was as if God Himself was speaking.

Ahithophel was much more than simply a highly acclaimed adviser to David; he was a close personal friend. In Psalm 55:12–14, David complained about someone who had turned against him:

> For it is not an enemy who taunts me—then I could bear it; it
> is not an adversary who deals insolently with me— then I could
> hide from him. But it is you, a man, my equal, my companion,
> my familiar friend.

Is this Ahithophel? It certainly seems so. Notice what else David said about him: "We used to take sweet counsel together; within God's house we walked in the throng." David remembered worshipping God together with this dear friend.

The thought of facing David also would have factored into his decision to take his own life. He knew that once the coup failed, he would stand before the king again, this time as a traitor rather than as a beloved friend and trusted counselor.

Dealing with Injustice

At some point, we all suffer unjustly at the hands of others and feel the desire to get revenge. Such feelings arise not only from injustices in our personal lives, but also from the actions of those in authority. There are also times when we think God isn't doing enough to correct the unfairness and evil in the world. We believe He's letting wickedness go unchecked, and we feel we must do something about it to "help" Him administer the needed justice.

This is why the account of Ahithophel remains relevant today. It warns of the tragic consequences that come from pursuing our own retribution. Not only did things end badly for him, but he advocated the same behavior he had objected to in David's life: adultery and murder. Ahithophel became the mirror image of the object of his hatred. In the end, his advice reflected the very sins that caused him to initially desire vengeance against the king.

This is an all-too-common outcome of hatred that remains unaddressed over time. Spiteful preoccupation with the object of our hatred is dangerous, because, more often than not, it transforms us into the very people we hate. In the end, we become just like them!

How, then, can we righteously deal with the injustices we suffer or see in the world? How do we guard against becoming like Ahithophel?

1. Trust God to Deal with Injustice

Was God highly displeased with David's sin with Bathsheba? Absolutely! It wasn't something He overlooked, not at all. The king paid a steep price for his sin, even after he repented. The child born as the result of his adultery died, and afterward David suffered greatly as he watched violence erupt in his family. He endured years of painful consequences for his sin.

David sinned grievously against the Lord, but he also sought and received forgiveness for his actions (see Psalm 51).

Ahithophel, however, did not trust God to deal with the king's evil behavior. He wanted David to pay for it with his life, and Ahithophel wanted to be the one to administer the ultimate justice.

Paul gives specific guidance in regard to seeking revenge: Let God deal with it; trust Him regardless of what happens to us or what we see in the world. Romans 12:19 says, "Beloved, never avenge yourselves, but leave it to the wrath of God, for it is written, 'Vengeance is mine, I will repay, says the Lord.'" Even when someone has deeply injured or offended us, the apostle instructs us not to seek our own revenge, but to leave it in God's hands.

When we release the injustices we experience into God's hands, we demonstrate our dependence on Him. We trust that He sees what happened, loves us more than we can imagine, and will work everything out "for good" (Romans 8:28). Please know that others can't thwart God's sovereign purpose for our lives directly, indirectly, or in any other way.

Practically speaking, following the apostle's command spares us much inner turmoil. When we become consumed with seeking revenge, it always hurts us more than it does the object of our fury. It takes away our joy and peace, and rarely brings the satisfaction we think it will; it's hollow at best. That's what I felt vicariously as I watched the end of *The Count of Monte Cristo*. I wonder if Ahithophel felt this same emptiness of soul as he put the rope around his neck.

Sometimes a desire for vengeance springs from sources other than personal pain. We see wickedness and deception flourishing, and something inside us cries out for justice. For me, such anger rises the quickest when I read about the horrors of abortion and wonder why Congress doesn't stop the vile practices associated with it, such as the killing of children who survive abortions. "Why doesn't God intervene to put an end to this now?" I ask.

Yes, the Supreme Court has overturned *Roe v. Wade*, but the passion for killing innocent children remains high in the US government and in many states. In addition, the war against our children goes far beyond killing them in the womb.

What do we do when our souls cry out for justice?

For me, Psalm 37 draws my heart back to trusting God's wisdom regardless of the evil I see in the nation and around the world. I meditate on the advice David gave in Psalm 37:7–9:

> Be still before the Lord and wait patiently for him; fret not yourself over the one who prospers in his way, over the man who carries out evil devices! Refrain from anger, and forsake wrath! Fret not yourself; it tends only to evil. For the evildoers shall be cut off, but those who wait for the Lord shall inherit the land.

When I read, for the two hundredth time or more, the words of this psalm, I remember the Lord sees what I see (and much, much more). He will someday correct all injustice in a fair manner. The psalmist tells us to relax; the Lord remains sovereign over all things. No one will ever get away with the wickedness, deception, and violence they perpetrate against us and others.

I also contemplate the Lord's mercy and remember His extreme forbearance in dealing with my sins over the course of my life. Where would I be apart from the Lord's over-the-top patience? What if He were not merciful to me? I shudder to think what might have happened if that were not the case.

2. Thank the Lord for Not Giving Us What We Deserve

In the midst of our righteous indignation, it's easy to forget how much God has forgiven us. Psalm 130:3 says, "If you, O Lord, should mark iniquities, O Lord, who could stand?" Apart from the saving work of Christ, we all face eternal condemnation for our sins regardless of how inconsequential they might seem. Despite our despicable record of sins, we stand righteous in His sight (Ephesians 1:3–14).

As Ahithophel became absorbed with David's sin, he overlooked two essential truths. First, he lost sight of God's abundant grace and mercy in forgiving his many sins. Second, he failed to fully grasp the seriousness of his sins against the Lord. Although it's likely that he never committed adultery or directly caused the killing of another person, his sins amounted to grievous offences that required God's forgiveness just as David's transgressions had.

How often do we forget these things in our zeal to avenge a wrong or lash out at the inequalities we see?

If David was referring to Ahithophel in Psalm 55:14—and it's almost certain he was—then the two men had worshipped God together at the tabernacle. Ahithophel knew Scripture and believed in the Lord. However, he became consumed with the same self-righteousness that affects so many of us today: He saw his friend's sins as being far weightier than those he had committed. This blinded him to God's forgiving mercy—in which both he and David had approached the Lord during the times they worshipped together.

Properly recognizing the serious nature of our own sins, which God has already freely and completely forgiven, diminishes our desire for vengeance on those who wrong us. When we remember that God in His mercy has given us the very righteousness of Jesus (2 Corinthians 5:21), we realize His forgiveness of our wrongdoing is so much greater than the offenses He asks us to forgive.

Luke recounts what happened when a Pharisee named Simon invited Jesus to a dinner party (Luke 7:36–50). Not long after they had reclined at the table for the meal, a woman identified only as a "sinner" went to Jesus and began washing His feet with her tears and wiping them dry with her hair. She also anointed His feet with oil.

Simon became incensed that Jesus allowed this sinner, who was a prostitute, to touch Him. Simon responded with righteous indignation, likely quite similar to what Ahithophel felt. If Jesus were a prophet, the Pharisee reasoned, He would condemn the woman for her shameful past. Simon demanded an immediate and just response to her sinfulness.

Instead, Jesus told a parable to illustrate the relationship between the intensity of our love for Him and the degree of forgiveness we receive. The underlying point of Jesus' story was that He has already forgiven all of His followers so very much, and an accurate understanding of what He has already done for us should increase our love for Him and compel us to be more generous in showing mercy toward others.

We have all received abundant forgiveness and steadfast love from God.

The sins of others may appear more obvious than ours, as was the case of the woman who approached Jesus. However, regardless of the severity of our wrongdoing (by human standards), apart from Christ, our sins make all of us "children of wrath" before God intervenes to redeem us (Ephesians 2:3). It defines us before we receive the gifts of faith and eternal life (see Ephesians 2:8–9).

When we put our faith in Jesus, He wipes the slate clean. He forgives all our sins, including those we have yet to commit. *His mercy and grace know no bounds.*

When I feel an urge to get even with someone, and that does happen, I focus on Jesus' patience with me and His total forgiveness of all my sins. During the years I resisted His love, He waited for me to return to Him. His patience, along with the recognition of my current tendency toward sin, often negates my desire for revenge, although sometimes it takes a while for this mindset to totally relieve my mind of such thoughts.

Those who mistakenly believe God has forgiven them "little" not only struggle in their love of God, but also refuse to show mercy to others. This is a lesson I must continue to remind myself; it's perhaps the most significant take-away from this book.

Walking with God

What does Ahithophel teach us about our walk with God? His behavior demonstrates our need to trust the Lord when others injure us or when we see evil and lawlessness flourish.

Walking with the Lord means we remain ever mindful of the Gospel when feelings of revenge surface. We must never forget the gravity of our own sins when considering the behavior of others. Jesus' forgiveness means we won't spend eternity in Hell. How is it that we so often diminish the significance of our own sins and amplify the weight of the sins of those around us?

As followers of Jesus, we rest secure in Him, just as the words of Colossians 2:13–14 assure us:

You, who were dead in your trespasses and the uncircumcision of your flesh, God made alive together with him, having forgiven us all our trespasses, by canceling the record of debt that stood against us with its legal demands. This he set aside, nailing it to the cross.

The Lord has forever nailed our sins—past, present, and future—to the cross.

Those who are secure in their relationship with Christ face no possibility of condemnation (Romans 8:1, 31–39). *Wow! God's grace is beyond amazing!*

How can we seek revenge against those who have wronged us when we remember the incredible love of God, through which He has completely forgiven all of our sins—every last one? More than that, Jesus is preparing a place for us in Heaven and is coming soon to take us there (John 14:1–3).

This doesn't mean we shouldn't speak out against evil or refuse to take action to counter wrongdoing. There may be a time when we must protest against horrors like abortion, sex trafficking, and the LBGTQ assault on our children.

However, as we take advantage of all the opportunities the Lord gives us to do so, we must allow His love and grace to dictate our words and our actions, fully understanding that "but by the grace of God, so go I."

STUDY GUIDE

Chapter 5

Ahithophel: The King's Advisor Who Sought Revenge

Passages: 2 Samuel 16:15–23; 17:1–23; Psalm 55:12–14
Key verses: Romans 12:17–18; Psalm 130:3; Luke 7:36–50

Questions for discussion:

1. What's the most likely motive behind Ahithophel's effort to join Absalom in his coup to remove David as king of Israel?
2. What evidence do we see in 2 Samuel 15:12 that Ahithophel knew of Absalom's plan in advance and was ready to join him?
3. What advice did Ahithophel give Absalom? How does it reveal a hidden danger that arises from intensely hating another person?
4. What thoughts may have prompted Ahithophel to commit suicide?
5. Why can we trust God to deal with the injustice we experience as well as that which we see in our world?
6. How might the story and parable recorded in Luke 7:36–50 help us deal with desires for revenge? Who are the ones God has "forgiven much"?
7. Is there a time for righteous anger about sin? Why is it important to quickly deal with these feelings, too?

STUDY GUIDE

Chapter 5

8. How does the message of the Gospel help relieve our desires to get even with others that wrong us?

9. What impacts you the most from the story of this little-known character?

Key lesson: Walking with the Lord means we remain ever mindful of the Gospel when feelings of revenge surface within us. We need never forget the seriousness of our own sins when we're looking at the offences of others.

6

REHOBOAM

THE WISE KING'S SON WHO MADE A FOOLISH DECISION

*The beginning of wisdom is this: Get wisdom, and whatever
you get, get insight. Prize her highly, and she will exalt you; she
will honor you if you embrace her. She will place on your head a
graceful garland; she will bestow on you a beautiful crown.*

—PROVERBS 4:7–9

History is full of people who have made foolish decisions. Many of these blunders dramatically altered the course of events and influenced a great many lives. Napoleon Bonaparte's invasion of Russia proved to be disastrous for both him and his army. In a matter of months, he lost half a million soldiers because of the ensuing war, typhus infections, food shortages, and freezing temperatures. Russian soldiers later escorted Napoleon's remaining one hundred thousand soldiers back to France.

Do you remember the story of the Trojan horse? Although historians remain divided as to whether it was an actual event or fiction, even as legend it conveys the necessity of making wise decisions. In his book,

The Iliad, Homer tells the story of the lengthy battle for the city of Troy and the Greek's "gift," the Trojan horse, offered to the people of the city.

After besieging the city of Troy for ten years without success, the Greeks devised an ingenious plan to defeat their longtime foe. They built a wooden horse large enough to fit a dozen soldiers inside. They then wheeled it to the gate of the city of Troy and pretended to withdraw their army from the city.

The people of Troy, thinking they had finally outlasted the enemy, opened the gate and accepted what they believed to be a gift from the retreating Greek army. In the middle of the night, the soldiers came out from hiding inside the horse and opened the gates of the city. The Greek army, which had earlier withdrawn only until they were just out of sight, rushed into Troy through the open gates and easily captured the city.

In the Old Testament, we find the record of another foolish decision that changed the course of history for the nation of Israel. Rehoboam, the son of King Solomon, spurned the requests of those he served. Instead, he followed the disastrous counsel of his young advisers.

What led to his reckless acceptance of terrible advice? What caused him to so rudely dismiss the desires of the people of Israel who had come to make him king?

Rehoboam: The Formative Years

We find many of the answers to these questions in the early, formative years of Rehoboam. His father, though initially a godly and wise king, later joined his pagan wives in worshipping their false gods. First Kings 11:4 says:

> When Solomon was old his wives turned away his heart after other gods, and his heart was not wholly true to the Lord his God, as was the heart of David his father.

Solomon built a temple east of Jerusalem for the god of the Ammonites, referred to as both "Milcom" and "Molech" in Scripture (1 Kings 11:5–8). He commissioned idolatrous temples for his other wives as well, but the verse in 1 Kings 11 uses the temple of the Ammonite god as an example of the king's construction program for his foreign wives. Solomon apparently favored his Ammonite wife, for not only did he erect a temple where she could worship her god, but he also chose her son to be the next king of Israel. Second Chronicles 12:13 identifies Rehoboam's mother as "Naamah the Ammonite."

Immediately after identifying Naamah as Rehoboam's mother, the writer says about Rehoboam: "And he did evil, for he did not set his heart to seek the Lord" (2 Chronicles 12:14). The woman who turned Solomon's heart away from the Lord raised a son who never learned how to walk with the Lord or seek His wisdom.

Rehoboam's idolatrous mother wasn't the only influence on him during his early years. Second Chronicles 12:13 says Rehoboam was forty-one when he became king following the forty-year reign of his father. Before taking the throne, Rehoboam spent almost his entire life as the cherished son of the wealthiest monarch in the world at that time, as well as ever since then (1 Kings 10:23). As Solomon's son, Rehoboam never experienced anything apart from a life of fabulous wealth, luxury, extravagance, and indulgence.

It's just like the theme of many movies, especially those from 1930 to 1960. The son of a wealthy father turns out to be a bum, to put it nicely. His life of ease and riches renders him useless in dealing with the realities of life. Such was the case with Rehoboam; his life as the favored son of King Solomon caused him to depend on his enormous wealth rather than on God. As a result, he was unable to wisely respond to the pleas of the Israelites who came to make him king.

When faced with change that threatened his life of privilege, limitless indulgence, and pleasure, he chose the path most likely to preserve it. He didn't seek God's wisdom when he needed it the most.

The Fateful Decision

When King Solomon died, the people of Israel came to Shechem to make Rehoboam their king. Because of their strong reservations about him, they made a request of Rehoboam: "Your father made our yoke heavy. Now therefore lighten the hard service of your father and his heavy yoke on us, and we will serve you" (2 Chronicles 10:4). The demand seemed quite reasonable; it was a small price for Rehoboam to pay in order to become king of the most powerful and wealthiest nation in the ancient world.

Unfortunately, Rehoboam saw the appeal as a threat to his extravagant lifestyle. He asked for three days to consider their demand. The delay, however, gave time for the rebellion against him to grow. The people likely sensed that Rehoboam's hesitation meant he would continue the harsh treatment of his father.

Solomon didn't make slaves out of the Israelites, at least not on a permanent basis. However, he did draft many into lengthy service as laborers (1 Kings 9:22–23). When he had built the Temple, he had conscripted thousands of Hebrew people to help with its construction (1 Kings 5:13–18). Solomon had also built a fabulous palace for himself, and we can safely assume he relied on the Hebrews for the needed labor for that as well.

Based on the complaints of the people after Solomon's reign, forcibly drafting Israelites for lavish building programs seems to have continued long after he finished those projects. All the hard labor took a heavy toll on the workers, and they understandably demanded relief.

During the three-day delay he had requested, Rehoboam consulted the elders who had served his father. They instructed him to "be kind" and give a "favorable answer" to the people (2 Chronicles 10:6–7, NIV). The account in 1 Kings 12:7 tells us Solomon's advisers urged Rehoboam to be a servant to the people. If he did that, the people would serve him.

Rehoboam apparently didn't like the sound of serving others. He rejected the wise counsel of the elders and discussed the matter with the young men with whom he had grown up. Many scholars believe these advisers were the other sons of Solomon. That would explain their motive for wanting Solomon's extravagant practices to continue. Along with Rehoboam, they would benefit from the continuation of their father's policies. Their lives of luxury would thus move forward unimpeded.

The younger group told Rehoboam to assert his forcefulness by letting the people know he would be tougher than his father. They advised him to say: "My little finger is thicker than my father's thighs" (2 Chronicles 10:10). In other words, his strength in imposing his will on them would be even greater than that of Solomon.

In addition, they recommended that Rehoboam also threaten them with the following words: "My father disciplined you with whips, but I will discipline you with scorpions" (2 Chronicles 10:11). Can you imagine hearing promises of such harsh treatment from a presidential candidate and then voting for him? Neither can I.

How could Rehoboam have even imagined the people would make him king after he proclaimed he would inflict much physical harm on them if they didn't obey him? What was he thinking?

When the Israelites returned to Shechem, Rehoboam delivered the cruel words recommended by his contemporaries. His impertinent reply did not impress the people at all. The ten northern tribes of Israel rebelled against him and chose Jeroboam to be their king. Only Judah and Benjamin remained loyal to the house of David and gave Rehoboam their throne (2 Chronicles 10:12–19). God's continuing grace to King David and his covenant kept the tribes of Judah and Benjamin devoted to Rehoboam.

Because of his reckless decision, Rehoboam lost a significant portion of his kingdom. The fertile hills and valleys of Samaria and Galilee now belonged to the Northern Kingdom. The rich lands across the Jordan River were also gone. He lost much of the splendor of his father's realm.

This outcome came directly from the Lord as the result of Solomon's sins. Second Chronicles 10:15 says:

So the king did not listen to the people, for it was a turn of affairs brought about by God that the Lord might fulfill his word, which he spoke by Ahijah the Shilonite to Jeroboam the son of Nebat.

God worked His sovereign will through Rehoboam's foolish decision. This, however, didn't relieve Rehoboam of his responsibility in the matter. Such unwise choices characterized his entire life. He never sought the Lord for advice, except when it became expedient to give the *appearance* that he was doing so.

A Pretense of Obedience

After Israel split into two nations, Rehoboam prospered for a few years as king of the southern tribes of Judah and Benjamin. When Jeroboam instituted idol worship for the northern ten tribes, many of the priests and Levites refused to take part and returned to Jerusalem, thus strengthening Rehoboam's hold on the Southern Kingdom (2 Chronicles 11:13–17).

Unfortunately, Rehoboam's initial obedience to the Lord proved to be short-lived and only a pretense. Second Chronicles 12:1 tells us: "When the rule of Rehoboam was established and strong, he abandoned the law of the Lord, and all Israel with him." When he needed the Lord to establish his rule, he appeared to walk with Him. Once Rehoboam sensed his kingdom was secure, he quickly abandoned Him.

Because Rehoboam turned his heart away from God, He sent Shishak, king of Egypt, against him. Shishak is known in Egyptian history as Sheshonk I, the energetic pharaoh and founder of Egypt's Twenty-second Dynasty. King Shishak I left a record of his conquests of Judah and Israel, carving into a wall of his temple a list of cities he conquered, which remains visible today.

History tells us Shishak's main purpose in conquering other nations was to plunder their wealth rather than expand his political rule. This explains why Rehoboam remained king, although he was subservient to the Egyptian ruler.

As Shishak's armies advanced on Jerusalem, Rehoboam, along with the "princes of Israel," heeded the warning of a prophet and humbled himself before the Lord. God responded to his short-lived change of heart and did not allow the Egyptian king to destroy Jerusalem (2 Chronicles 12:2–8).

Service to Shishak, however, did not alter the trajectory of Rehoboam's life. The final assessment of his reign is that he was an evil king who "did not set his heart to seek the Lord" (2 Chronicles 12:14). His foolish decisions flowed out of a heart that did not trust the Lord or seek His wisdom. His humility in the face of danger quickly ended after the Lord removed His hand of judgment from Judah.

Making Wise Decisions

During the early months of 2016, I finalized my decision to retire early and become a full-time writer. I prayed frequently about it and, over time, became convinced that God was leading me in that direction.

For many years, I had written adult Sunday school curriculum for the David C. Cook Christian publishing company. I loved writing, and my passion to do it full time intensified as I contemplated the prospect of retiring early.

During this time of seeking the Lord's direction for my future, I received an assignment from Cook to write the Bible study sections of two lessons from the book of Judges covering God's calling of Barak and Gideon. As I was writing, God spoke to my heart: "Have I not called you as well?" Like Gideon, I knew if I followed the Lord's call, He would need to be with me in a remarkable way. I thought of Barak leading ten thousand soldiers down Mount Tabor to confront Sisera and his deadly chariots (Judges 4:14–15). Barak took his army into battle knowing the Lord would show up and rout his enemy. If not, they faced certain disaster.

My decision in 2016 entailed risks that continue to this day. I am still uncertain where this path will take me or how God will provide for my needs along the way. It was—and remains—a step of faith.

We all desire to make wise decisions. So often, however, in the rush of daily life, we fail to take most matters to the Lord—except for the "critical" ones such as marriage or employment. As we saw with King Rehoboam, poor decision-making is the result of never learning to seek the Lord or trust Him. With that in mind, what considerations might prepare us for the times we need to make good decisions on important matters?

1. Is the Well-being of Others a Factor?

Amy Morin, speaker and author of *13 Things Mentally Strong People Don't Do*, wrote a short article for *Forbes* magazine titled "5 Phrases That Signal You're About to Make a Bad Decision." According to Morin, the first sign that we're about to make a poor decision is when personal happiness becomes a prime consideration.[8] This sounds like Rehoboam, doesn't it? He wanted the pleasures he had enjoyed while he was growing up to continue. His devotion to personal happiness laid the foundation for his unwise decisions.

Morin stated that another indicator of a poor choice is a lack of regard for others.[9] Rehoboam demonstrated this when he spurned those who came to make him king. His only thoughts consisted of what mattered to *him*, which led him to foolishly reject the Israelites' valid concerns.

When confronted with His disciples' quest for their own glory, Jesus responded with the following words recorded in Mark 10:43–45:

Whoever would be great among you must be your servant, and whoever would be first among you must be slave of all. For even the Son of Man came not to be served but to serve, and to give his life as a ransom for many.

Jesus wants our overriding concern to be serving others. He exemplified this attitude when He died in our place on the cross. In contrast to Rehoboam, Jesus asks us to serve both Him and others.

Happiness isn't bad; nor is it something we must try to avoid—not at all. One fruit of the Spirit is joy. I love and very much enjoy my life as an author. God doesn't seek to lead us down paths that lead to misery and despair. He takes us through tough times for our own good—both now and in the eternity He has planned for us.

Our motivation is key when we're making decisions. If our only consideration is our own pleasure and happiness without thinking of how our choices might impact others, chances are high that we will choose the wrong path.

2. Are We Routinely Taking Time to Seek the Lord's Leading?

Rehoboam's foolish decision in response to the Israelites' desires wasn't an isolated event; it flowed out of a lifetime of never seeking the Lord's wisdom or looking to Him for direction. Even when he appeared to be walking with the Lord, Rehoboam did so solely as a pretense to get what he wanted.

A peculiar incident during Rehoboam's reign further illustrates his hypocrisy. When Shishak, king of Egypt, went against Jerusalem, he plundered the treasures of the king's house, including the gold shields made during the reign of Solomon (2 Chronicles 12:9). Gold shields were much too heavy to carry into battle; instead, kings used them to display the wealth of their kingdom on special occasions.

After Shishak took the gold shields, Rehoboam replaced them with bronze ones (2 Chronicles 12:10–11). When used in religious ceremonies of the day, under the shining sun, the bronze armor gave the impression that no loss had occurred. In reality, the shields, like the worship of Rehoboam, were counterfeit. For much of his life, the king's devotion to God was a pretense that did not change his heart or alter the course of his life.

Making wise decisions is not about turning to the Lord only when we face crucial decisions. They more often flow out of a consistent pattern of seeking Him with all our heart. When this becomes a way of life, our decision-making ability improves, and we naturally take the time to prayerfully consider significant choices that lie ahead.

3. Are We Consistently Spending Time in God's Word?

At a critical point in Rehoboam's reign, we read: "When the rule of Rehoboam was established and he was strong, he abandoned the law of the Lord" (2 Chronicles 12:1). The king consulted Scripture only when it suited him; when his circumstances changed for the better, he quickly dispensed with his sham of being devoted to God's Word.

Rehoboam may have had a basic understanding of the five books of Moses, but he never knew the Lord, nor did he have a saving relationship with Him. That made him quick to cast aside any Scripture that conflicted with his own self-interests or popularity.

We have a distinct advantage over Rehoboam: the Holy Spirit living inside us to guide us as we meditate on God's Word. He not only gives us understanding of what we read, but He also uses its wisdom to guide us in our everyday lives. The Holy Spirit makes Scripture come alive—both as we study it and when we face challenging situations.

Do you regularly spend time in God's Word? If so, you're giving the Spirit much to work with in shaping your daily life as well as the course of your future! Wise decisions don't just happen; they flow out of the lives of people who continually spend time with the Lord through prayer and Bible study. According to the earlier-mentioned final assessment of Rehoboam's reign, this is something the self-absorbed king never did.

Many people today follow the example of Rehoboam. They cast aside portions of the Bible that don't fit their lifestyle, that interfere with their pursuit of happiness, or that make them less popular.

Such an approach to God's Word puts us on the same downward path Rehoboam traveled before he rebuffed the needs of the Israelites.

Walking with God

What does King Rehoboam teach us about our walk with God? His example reminds us that wise decisions flow out of having a close relationship with the Lord and an understanding of Scripture. The king's disastrous decision followed a lifetime of chasing after pleasure rather than following the Lord and caring about the needs of others.

Though abundantly foolish, Rehoboam's response to the people is not surprising, given his pattern of ignoring what really matters. He lived with no thought of eternity or regard for the wisdom that comes from knowing the Lord. Rehoboam reminds us that sound decisions can flow only from hearts enriched with God's Word and in tune with the Holy Spirit.

STUDY GUIDE

Chapter 6

Rehoboam: The Wise King's Son Who Made a Foolish Decision

Passages: 1 Kings 11:4–8; 12:1–24; 2 Chronicles 10:1–19
Key verses: Proverbs 4:7–9; Mark 10;43–45

Questions for discussion:

1. How did Solomon's support of his wives' idolatry lead to the divided kingdom of Israel?
2. How might Rehoboam's life before he became king have contributed to his foolish decision?
3. What motives might Rehoboam's young counselors have had for their poor advice?
4. How did making bronze shields illustrate Rehoboam's lack of genuineness during the times he sought to walk with the Lord?
5. What role do our motives play in our ability to make good decisions?
6. What type of intentions typically lead to choosing poor paths?
7. How does a thorough knowledge of God's Word contribute to our skill in making sound choices?
8. Why is it so necessary to spend time with the Lord?
9. Do you feel better equipped to make wise choices after reading the story of Rehoboam? Why or why not?

STUDY GUIDE

Chapter 6

Key lesson: Rehoboam's example reminds us that wise decisions flow out of a close walk with the Lord and daily dependence on and knowledge of Scripture. Rehoboam's disastrous decision resulted from a lifetime of seeking pleasure rather than the Lord.

King Rehoboam's life demonstrated a total allegiance to temporal realities with no thought of his life in eternity.

7

GEHAZI

THE PROPHET'S SERVANT WHO CHASED AFTER WEALTH

Do not lay up for yourselves treasures on earth, where moth and
rust destroy and where thieves break in and steal, but lay up
for yourselves treasures in heaven, where neither moth nor rust
destroys and where thieves do not break in and steal. For where
your treasure is, there your heart will be also.

—MATTHEW 6:19–21

The title instantly intrigued me: *Hot Tub Religion*. I found it on a table of discounted books at a local Christian bookstore. For three dollars, the book seemed like a terrific bargain, especially since one of my favorite theologians, J. I. Packer, had written it.

It exceeded my expectations!

Although it was written over twenty-five years ago, the book's title sums up how the modern quest for pleasure has infiltrated the modern Church, where materialism remains a significant problem—both inside and outside its fold.

The book came about as a result of Packer's experience in a hot tub one afternoon. He instantly saw parallels between relaxing in the soothing, swirling warm water and believers who elevate comfort above everything else, especially their relationship with God.

As with many other things, the problem is not so much with our desire for pleasure, but with the accompanying attitudes of our heart. Packer observed:

> Pleasure (conscious enjoyment) has no intrinsic moral quality. What makes pleasures right, good, and valuable or wrong, bad, and sinful is what goes with them. Look at the motivation and outcome of your pleasures. How hard do you chase after them?[10]

Just as the Apostle Paul wrote in 1 Timothy 6:10, it's the "love of money" that leads people astray. This brings us to the next character in our study, Gehazi, who literally chased after Naaman to acquire some of the Syrian's wealth. Infected with greed, he pursued what he thought would increase his enjoyment. Like so many, he desired the comfort and status money can bring.

For Gehazi and those like him, the problem rarely arises from what one does or does not have. As Packer points out, the more important issue rests in the motivation of our heart. The key consideration is our fondness of money and the pleasure that comes from having more of it. That's what caused Gehazi to chase after wealth.

A Servant of Elisha

Gehazi first appears in Scripture as the loyal servant of the prophet Elisha. Second Kings 4:8–37 presents the account of a wealthy Shunammite woman who convinced her husband to set aside a room in their home so Elisha could stay with them each time he visited the area. She extended this gesture of hospitality to Gehazi, a servant of the prophet, as well.

Grateful for the woman's kindness, Elisha asked one day if he could do her a favor. Her reply reflected the deep nature of her contentment; she couldn't think of anything to request. Still wanting to do something for her, Elisha later conferred with his servant about the matter. Gehazi pointed out the couple was childless and her husband was "old," making it unlikely they could conceive a child.

The prophet liked the idea and asked Gehazi to summon the woman. After telling her she would be holding a son in her arms within a year's time, she responded, "No, my lord, O man of God; do not lie to your servant" (2 Kings 4:16). Her reply indicated that she had been frustrated in the past by her desire to bear a child; she didn't want to face disappointment again. However, just as Elisha promised, she gave birth to a son the following year (2 Kings 4:17).

Years later, while working alongside his father in the field, the woman's son became ill and died. Understandably distraught, she asked the prophet for help. As she drew near, Elisha sent Gehazi to inquire about her well-being. The woman, however, refused to confide in the servant; she waited to confront Elisha with the dreadful news (2 Kings 4:18–28).

Once he heard the report, Elisha gave Gehazi his own staff and told him to go place the staff on the dead child. The child, however, did not respond.

In the meantime, the woman and the prophet were also traveling to the place where the child lay (2 Kings 4:29–31). When they arrived, Elisha went into the room where the child was and closed the door, allowing only Gehazi to be with him. As the prophet stretched out his body on the child, the boy came back to life (2 Kings 4:32–37).

In this sequence of events, Gehazi appears to be a trusted and loyal assistant to Elisha. The prophet had sought his advice and even sent him ahead to participate in raising the Shunammite's dead son. The woman, however, preferred to stay close to Elisha and confided only in him. She may have already recognized the character flaw in Gehazi that later became apparent.

Greed Overcomes Gehazi

Second Kings 5 records the story of the healing of Naaman, the commander of the armed forces of Syria. The stories of Elisha's miracles in
Israel reached the ears of Naaman through a servant girl he had taken
captive during an earlier conquest of Israel. The girl later testified to
her mistress regarding Elisha's healing power: "Would that my lord were
with the prophet who is in Samaria! He would cure him of his leprosy"
(2 Kings 5:3).

Acting on the girl's word, Naaman obtained permission from the king
of Syria to travel to Israel. He took along "ten talents of silver, six thousand
shekels of gold, and ten changes of clothing" to use to reward Elisha for
curing him (2 Kings 5:5). He believed the prophet would heal his leprosy.

Naaman found Elisha, and, after an initial reluctance, followed
the prophet's instructions by washing in the Jordan River. After he had
dipped himself in the river seven times as the prophet directed, the Lord
restored Naaman's flesh so it was like that "of a little child, and he was
clean" (2 Kings 5:14). After his healing, he returned to the prophet and
demonstrated his great appreciation by offering him the valuable gifts he
had brought. Elisha refused to accept the generous rewards from Naaman and sent him "in peace" back to Syria (2 Kings 5:19).

Naaman's response to Elisha indicates that a change also took place
in his heart. "Behold, I know that there is no God in all the earth but in
Israel; so accept now a present from your servant" (2 Kings 5:15). His
healing convinced him Elisha's God was the true and living Lord of all
the earth, so Naaman put his trust in Him.

Naaman also told the prophet he would not offer a sacrifice to any
god except the Lord. He apologized for the necessity of going into the
house of the Syrian god, a requirement of his official duties to the Syrian king. He hoped Elisha would understand he had no alternative
(2 Kings 5:17–18). Naaman's request displayed a sincere belief in the
God of Israel. He returned to Syria a changed man, one who now saw
futility of the pagan worship in his homeland.

As Naaman departed, Gehazi focused on Elisha's refusal to accept the gifts rather than on the commander's newfound faith. He believed his master had let Naaman off too easy by rejecting his generous offer of so many presents (2 Kings 5:20). He justified his greed by reasoning that Elisha had unnecessarily kept the Syrian commander from doing what was right.

Without Elisha's knowledge, Gehazi pursued Naaman. Imagine the sight of Gehazi running to catch up with Naaman, hoping to obtain something for himself. During his trek, he created a story, a lie, about how a need had suddenly arisen among the "sons of the prophets" (2 Kings 5:19–23). As a result of this late development, Gehazi said, Elisha had sent him to get a talent of silver and some changes of clothing.

Naaman gave Gehazi two talents of silver instead of one, along with the garments. He also provided two of his servants to help Gehazi carry the treasure, since each talent could weigh as much as 120 pounds.

Gehazi, however, sent the servants back to Naaman before they reached Elisha. It must have taken a strenuous effort for Gehazi to singlehandedly get the silver to his home. He foolishly thought he could hide his behavior from Elisha (2 Kings 5:24).

However, the length of time Gehazi had served Elisha should have been more than enough for him to realize he couldn't conceal his actions from the prophet. Elisha knew the truth, and gave Gehazi a chance to confess his sin, but he lied.

Grieved by his servant's behavior, Elisha explained that God had revealed everything to him. As judgment for his sin, Elisha said, Naaman's leprosy would rest upon Gehazi and his descendants (2 Kings 5:25–27).

The prophet affirmed that at times it's appropriate to accept such gifts. As we saw earlier, Elisha had welcomed the use of a special room where he and Gehazi could stay when they were visiting the area. Under different circumstances, they might not have refused Naaman's gifts, but this wasn't such an occasion.

Gehazi's Continued Service

We would expect this to be the end of Gehazi's service to Elisha. He had deliberately misrepresented the prophet, acquired goods that didn't belong to him, and lied to both Naaman and Elisha. After Elisha exposed his sin, Gehazi left the presence of the prophet as a leper. How could he continue to assist Elisha? Evidence exists, however, that indicates this incident did not end Gehazi's service to the prophet.

Later, as recorded in 2 Kings 8:3–6, we find Gehazi in the presence of the king of Israel. In the midst of Gehazi telling the king about all the great things Elisha had done, the Shunammite woman came before the king to plead her case regarding land someone had taken from her. Gehazi interceded; consequently, the king restored all her land to her.

Because it's doubtful that a leper would have been allowed in the presence of the king, a few commentators believe this incident happened before the account of Naaman's healing. Others, however, suggest that while the Syrian commander suffered from a skin disease, it was not what we refer to today as "leprosy"—Hansen's disease—which slowly deteriorates the flesh and leads to a slow and painful death.

If Naaman and later Gehazi suffered from a skin condition far less serious than Hansen's disease, it explains why Naaman had continued to serve as the commander of the Syrian army after contracting the ailment. It also helps us understand why the pronouncement was made upon Gehazi included his descendants. However, had the Lord inflicted him with Hansen's disease, he would have had no hope whatsoever of finding a wife and having children.

Since, as many believe, Gehazi's intercession for the Shunammite woman took place after Elisha exposed Gehazi's greed, it indicates he had repented and continued to serve the prophet. However, there's no suggestion that Gehazi followed in Elisha's footsteps as Elisha had done after God took his master, Elijah, to Heaven.

Serving the Right Master

Being content always comes down to who or what we serve, not what we possess. Jesus said, "No one can serve two masters, for either he will hate the one and love the other, or he will be devoted to the one and despise the other. You cannot serve God and money" (Matthew 6:24). The Greek word for "money" is *mammon*, as translated in the King James Version. The word primarily denotes money, but can also signify any possession that usurps the role of Jesus as Lord.

At its root, greed springs from choosing to serve what we have rather than the Lord; it's never a matter of how much or how little we own.

The following considerations can help us remain faithful to the Lord and avoid Gehazi's problem with greed and its troublesome consequences.

1. Trust the Lord

There have been times when I've faced severe financial struggles. When I changed careers, my income did not match my expenses; it didn't even come close. As a result, I all but stopped setting aside money for the Lord.

The Lord impressed on my heart my need to start trusting Him again in the area of giving, but I resisted. With my recent graduate business degree, I remained confident something would soon open up. When that happened, I would start putting checks in the offering plates again.

The Lord, however, had a different sequence of events in mind for me.

After seeing my prayer request regarding my finances in my church's weekly bulletin, a man with a financial investment background invited me to his home for a talk. I described my situation in full detail, and he assured me I was doing everything right...except for one thing. He suggested I start giving again, starting at five percent of my income, and then see what the Lord might do.

I accepted his challenge. Earlier, I had sensed the Lord encouraging me through the words of Malachi 3:10 to "test" Him in the matter of giving. This time, rather than resist the Lord's promptings, I decided to follow them.

I also determined not to broadcast my dire financial situation to anyone. This matter was between the Lord and me; I would trust Him to provide rather than plead for others to help me. Several of my family members would have helped me in a heartbeat had they known about my circumstances, but I chose not to tell them.

During the first month of the test, I ran out of money before buying groceries, gas, and any other necessities. The next paycheck wouldn't come for two more weeks. My mom, not fully aware of my situation, "happened" to call and offer to send me money, which got me through the first month.

A similar shortfall occurred the second month. I had less than ten dollars in my pocket and bank account combined, and that was before I had taken care of the basics. But this time, the Lord began to change my circumstances.

My manager called me into his office on Monday of the first week of my financial deficit and offered me a temporary promotion so I could do technical writing for him. The three-dollar hourly increase in pay, he explained, had already begun the previous week and would also apply to any overtime. Before my temporary position ended, I applied for and received a permanent position, which gave me another significant pay raise.

I learned a valuable lesson from this: The Lord was willing to meet my needs as I demonstrated my trust in Him. My giving became a tangible way for me to display my confidence in Him during my time of financial need. There were many times when I didn't *feel* as though I was trusting Him, but giving to the Lord's work became a way to demonstrate my dependence on Him, even when my doubts begin to surface.

The first step in avoiding developing a greed like that of Gehazi is to trust the Lord. However, we must never think of giving as a way to *get* something from Him; that mindset shifts the focus back to us. We give from our resources to show we trust Him to meet our needs, then we wait for Him to act according to His sovereign will for our lives.

2. Look for Ways to Bless Others

Ephesians 4:28 has always intrigued me:

> Let the thief no longer steal, but rather let him labor, doing honest work with his own hands, so that he may have something to share with anyone in need.

Apparently, a few of the new converts in Ephesus didn't stop stealing after they turned to the Lord. The Greek word for "steal" doesn't denote being a professional thief; rather, it describes those who habitually take what doesn't belong to them.

Paul's command was for such people to work so they could give to rather than take from others. In other words, they were to be a blessing to others, especially their brothers and sisters in the Lord. A key purpose of work is to enable us to acquire resources to help others.

Greed, as we saw in the Gehazi's case, reverses that process. While he pretended to obtain the silver and changes of clothes so he could bless others, his real motive was to keep those things for himself.

During one tax season some time ago, I worked for an accounting firm helping prepare tax returns—documents that often clearly reveal one's financial priorities. I noticed several clients put away large sums of money for retirement, apparently with little thought of using it for the Lord's work or blessing others in the present.

It's certainly wise to plan for retirement; I don't fault anyone for doing that. However, many did so without regard for the less fortunate or for God's Kingdom.

God wants us to bless others with what we have and not hold on to our resources as a way to simply fulfill our own desires. Today, there are many options for giving in a way that blesses others spiritually or physically.

3. Learn the Secret of Contentment

John D. Rockefeller gained incredible wealth from his successes in the oil industry. When someone once asked him, "How much is enough?" Rockefeller responded, "One dollar more." Even as the richest person in the world at the time, he wasn't content with the amount of his vast wealth.

Paul's words in Philippians 4:11–12 offer a sharp contrast to Rockefeller's perspective on wealth. There, the apostle wrote:

> Not that I am speaking of being in need, for I have learned in whatever situation I am to be content. I know how to be brought low, and I know how to abound. In any and every circumstance, I have learned the secret of facing plenty and hunger, abundance and need.

Regardless of his circumstances, Paul knew the secret of contentment. What is this mystery of learning to be satisfied regardless of our station in life? Paul gave us the answer in verse 13 of Philippians 4: "I can do all things through him who strengthens me." Jesus was the source of his strength, regardless of what happened. Paul trusted Christ—whether or not he had enough to meet his needs. He rested in the Lord's strength and ability to provide for his well-being.

The contrast between the words of the Apostle Paul and those of Rockefeller confirms that contentment doesn't depend on what we have, but on our attitude about our possessions—and whom or what we serve. Paul's devotion to the Lord enabled him to feel content even when he lacked necessities. Rockefeller's dedication to money and power left him without satisfaction in spite of his enormous wealth.

4. Guard How Your Example Affects Others

There's one more thing we need to keep in mind as we seek to avoid the example of Gehazi. It may have been the most grievous result of his greed.

Commentators believe Elisha turned down Naaman's offer of riches because the Syrian general was new to the faith, and I agree. The prophet didn't want him to leave thinking his healing, or even his salvation, had resulted from his generous reward. Returning to Syria with all the lavish gifts he had taken to Israel would reinforce the extravagance of God's grace: He had done nothing to merit the great physical and spiritual blessings he had received from the Lord during his visit to Israel.

The problem wasn't in Elisha receiving the silver and clothing from Naaman, but in what accepting them might signify. As a new believer, Naaman might conclude the presents had "paid" for his healing. Worse yet, he might think they had something to do with "purchasing" eternal life.

In contrast to the attitude of the servant girl in Naaman's house who faithfully testified regarding God's healing power, Gehazi's behavior became a poor example of what it means to be a believer. His greed carried the danger of compromising the faith of the new believer, especially if Naaman had recognized the deceit behind Gehazi's sudden request for the silver and clothing. What might Naaman have thought when his servants reported that Gehazi sent them back before they delivered the gifts to Elisha? Did they know the gifts never reached Elisha?

We must consider that how we handle our finances affects others. Even if we don't broadcast our giving (as the Pharisees did), those around us notice our priorities regarding how we use our resources, even though we might not think they do.

Walking with God

What does Gehazi's greed teach us about our walk with God? It illustrates the danger of pursuing riches at the expense of devotion to the Savior.

Walking with the Lord means we worship Him alone rather than the pleasures we might obtain with money. Hebrews 13:5 says: "Keep your life free from love of money, and be content with what you have, for [the Lord] has said, 'I will never leave you nor forsake you.'" Doesn't this sum up all we need to know about materialism? Materialism affects the poor and rich alike, since it's never a matter of how much or how little we have. Contentment is the opposite of materialism.

Notice also the writer of Hebrews immediately followed up his command regarding the love of money with the promise that the Lord will "never leave...nor forsake" us. Regardless of our financial situation, we have the assurance of the Lord's unending presence; He alone gives us the strength to be content with what we have.

Satisfaction comes from trusting God's character and His plans. He will always be with us and give us the strength and provisions for whatever He calls us to do. We can count on that, regardless of our circumstances or financial standing.

STUDY GUIDE
Chapter 7

Gehazi: The Prophet's Servant Who Chased after Wealth

Passage: 2 Kings 4–5
Key verses: Matthew 6:19–34; Ephesians 4:28; Hebrews 13:5

Questions for discussion:

1. How does J. I. Packer's experience in the hot tub relate to the story of Gehazi?
2. What do we learn about Gehazi from before greed overcame him? Were there any warning signs of his later failure?
3. Do you think the servants of Naaman became suspicious of Gehazi when he sent them back before reaching Elisha? Why or why not?
4. Why was it so foolish for Gehazi to lie to the prophet?
5. How does giving to the Lord's work demonstrate our trust in Him?
6. How does Ephesians 4:28 relate to the motive behind how we manage our money?
7. Why did Elisha refuse to accept any of the gifts from Naaman? Why was that so important to the Syrian's understanding of his healing and newfound faith?
8. Why is the way we handle our money so important to how we can influence those who don't have a relationship with Christ?

STUDY GUIDE

Chapter 7

9. What does 1 Timothy 6:10 say about our relationship with money? How does it apply to us regardless of our financial situation?

Key lesson: The greed of Gehazi illustrates the danger of pursuing riches at the expense of our devotion to the Savior. On the other hand, we learn that contentment comes from trusting God's character and His purposes for our lives.

8

ESAU

THE SON WHO LIVED FOR THE MOMENT

If you remember that you have this wonderful future ahead of you, you won't live as if this moment is all you have and you will be free of the anxiety of fearing that somehow this moment will pass you by.

—PAUL DAVID TRIPP, *NEW MORNING MERCIES*

"Go ahead! Kiss me! Forget you're married to my sister!" That tagline from the 1942 movie, *In This Our Life*, highlights Bette Davis' role as a woman who lived exclusively for her own happiness at the expense of everyone around her, including her sister.

Shortly after the movie begins, Stanley (played by Bette Davis) runs away with her sister's husband and eventually marries him. However, the thrill-seeking Stanley never remains satisfied for any length of time. Her constant need for attention and reckless spending eventually drives her husband to drink and commit suicide.

In an amazing display of grace, Stanley's sister, Roy, comforts Stanley as she grieves the loss of her husband (who Stanley stole from Roy!).

111

Such kindness, however, does not deter Stanley from her destructive, pleasure-seeking path.

Later, driving drunk and much too fast, Stanley hits a mother and her young daughter as they cross a street. She craftily covers up her involvement in the fatal accident by casting blame on an innocent young man. As a result, a judge sentences him to jail for the rest of his life for the crime Stanley committed.

Eventually, Stanley's lust for happiness catches up with her as it becomes obvious that she was responsible for the death of the young girl. Stanley's life ends tragically as she flees from the police, still seeking a life devoid of consequences for her wicked behavior.

Esau suffered from the same shortsightedness as Stanley; he lived solely for the moment, for the instant satisfaction of his desires without regard for the Lord, His covenants, and eternity. We see his temporal perspective on life most clearly in his reckless sale of what should have been his most prized possession.

Selling His Birthright

The story began quite innocently. Esau, tired after a long day of hunting, came home experiencing what he later described as life-threatening hunger (Genesis 25:32). Moses simply tells us Esau was "exhausted" after spending hours in the fields chasing wild game (Genesis 25:29). In other contexts, this word implies hunger along with physical weariness, as was likely the case with Esau on that particular day.

Once he smelled Jacob's lentil stew, Esau demanded that his brother give him some. After his strenuous activities, this seemed to be the perfect way to renew his strength and satisfy his raging appetite. Jacob, sensing his brother's desperation, took advantage of him by asking Esau to sell him his birthright in return for the stew. Jacob may have desired the birthright for a long time and seized this opportunity to obtain it.

Esau confirmed the terms of the transaction with an oath, then ate and "went his way" (Genesis 25:29–34). The last phrase conveys the sense that he left unaware of the significance of what he had done. Scripture adds this comment at the end of verse 34: "Thus Esau despised his birthright."

A birthright was a prized possession in the days of Abraham and Isaac. It brought special benefits to the firstborn son and entitled him to the patriarch's blessing. In Esau's case, it included the blessings of the Abrahamic covenant. Isaac's heir would become the head of a great nation that would someday live in the Promised Land.

This covenant also entitled Isaac's son to a place in God's redemptive program, through which He would bless "all the families of the earth" (Genesis 12:3). The birthright thus gave Esau a place in God's plan to bring salvation to the entire world. Can you see why the Lord looked so negatively at Esau's careless disregard for it in return for momentary satisfaction of his hunger?

Hebrews 12:16 makes a powerful statement about Esau: "See that no one...is godless like Esau, who for a single meal sold his inheritance rights as the oldest son" (NIV). The word "godless" denotes someone who lives for temporal and material matters with no concern about spiritual values. Such people live as though God doesn't exist; they see nothing beyond this life. Doesn't this aptly describe all we know about Esau, who lived solely for the here and now with no thought of eternity?

Later, the result of Esau selling his birthright came to full fruition when Jacob stole Isaac's blessing from Esau.

Jacob Steals the Blessing of His Father

With the matter of the birthright forgotten, at least for the moment, Isaac decided it was time to bless Esau. The patriarch, thinking he was about to die (although he would live another forty-three years!), summoned his son and instructed him to hunt and prepare his father a meal of the game he caught (Genesis 27:1–4). In those days, people often marked solemn occasions, such as the conferring of the blessing, with a feast.

Isaac had at least three compelling reasons to bless Jacob rather than Esau. First, before the twins were born, the Lord had said "the older would serve the younger" (Genesis 25:23). This signified God's sovereign choice of Jacob over his older brother, as the Apostle Paul later expanded upon in Romans 9:10–13. This might explain Isaac's sense of terror after discovering he had been deceived (Genesis 27:33). The patriarch knew his plan to bless Esau contradicted God's instructions regarding his sons. He trembled when he recognized the Lord had sovereignly overruled his decision.

Second, Isaac certainly would have known about Esau's frivolous surrender of his birthright. In legal terms, it was a done deal. Jacob possessed a lawful claim to his father's blessing.

Third, Esau had demonstrated a lack of concern for spiritual matters by marrying ungodly Hittite women (Genesis 26:34–35). This alone should have caused Isaac to have second thoughts about blessing Esau. These wives had already brought much distress to both Isaac and his wife, Rebekah.

Isaac, aware of Esau's disdain for what truly mattered, went forward with his intent to bless Esau (Genesis 27:1–25). The thought of a great meal lured him into his foolish decision; he commented on how he loved eating "delicious food."

Genesis 25:28 not only reveals Isaac's "love" for Esau, but also that of Rebekah for Jacob; each had a favorite son. So, when she overheard Isaac's conversation with Esau regarding the blessing, Rebekah devised a plot for Jacob to obtain it instead. The quickness of her response and careful attention to details suggest she had planned for just such a scenario. Jacob readily went along with his mom's scheme, trusting deception rather than the Lord to obtain the blessing already promised to him.

Rebekah prepared two young goats, and Jacob, disguised as Esau, presented the meat to his father as if they were wild game. The ruse worked just as Rebekah intended, thanks in large measure to Isaac's blindness. Isaac ate the food, drank the wine, and asked for a kiss. Because Jacob was wearing Esau's clothes, he smelled like his brother. This convinced Isaac that he was blessing Esau.

While Jacob was going through with the elaborate deception, Esau prepared his meal in just the right manner for his father. He then brought the food in to Isaac and asked for his blessing. The reality of how Jacob had deceived him to obtain the blessing stunned Isaac and angered Esau (Genesis 27:33–41).

What might have happened if Jacob hadn't tricked his father? We will never know, but since God had already chosen Jacob to receive the blessing, I believe He would have overruled the intention of the aging patriarch to bless the older brother.

Esau complained bitterly about Jacob's ruse. The real tragedy, however, was Esau's disdain for what truly mattered. His obsession with his immediate needs blinded him to the eternal significance of his foolish disregard for his birthright. He failed to see anything beyond what was right in front of him.

Scripture doesn't provide any insight into Jacob's motive for deceiving his father. Later, however, we see that he treasured God's favor. Why else would he wrestle all night with the Lord to obtain His blessing (Genesis 32:22–32)? At least later in his life, Jacob saw something far more valuable in the blessing than his brother did. He may have already understood that when he purchased the birthright from Esau and later stole the blessing, but, again, the Bible doesn't tell us.

From our perspective, we clearly recognize Esau's earthbound, temporal perspective. As we contemplate his obsession with the moment, we gain valuable insight to help us avoid his shortsightedness.

Living Beyond the Moment

At critical times, Esau made terrible decisions because he couldn't see beyond the moment. Just like Stanley in the movie *In This Our Life*, he lived for the immediate gratification of his desires without any regard for the consequences, the future, or eternity.

Scripture describes him as being godless, with only a desire for material possessions and power without any thought for the Lord or what mattered to Him. As such, Esau's example alerts us to the dangers of living solely for the temporal world, for what we can see versus eternal realities (2 Corinthians 4:17–18).

Esau's example highlights various perils we must avoid if we want to please the Lord and make wise choices.

1. The Danger of Seeking Immediate Satisfaction

I wonder what made Esau's hunger so intense on the day he sold his birthright. It's difficult to believe he was actually as close to death as he claimed. Why couldn't he have waited for someone else to cook something for him? Was Jacob really such a great cook?

Later, Esau prepared a meal of "delicious food" for his father on the day he expected to receive his father's blessing (Genesis 27:31). So, Esau *could* cook! Had he really been too exhausted to do anything but beg Jacob for food in exchange for his birthright?

What did Esau do at other times when he returned from a day of hunting? Not only could he cook, but he was a member of a wealthy family. Although not specifically mentioned in Genesis, it's highly probable that his family had several servants who could have prepared him a meal.

I don't doubt Esau's weariness or extreme hunger. While it wouldn't have been the most satisfying choice at the time, he could have refused Jacob's deal and sought other alternatives. Why did he make such a rash decision?

Desire by itself is not bad or sinful. Imagine never being hungry or wanting tasty food. While that might be great for weight control, it could have fatal consequences. We need food to survive, and hunger keeps us pursuing needed nourishment.

However, when we seek immediate satisfaction of a desire, it most often results in foolish choices. Esau's decision to sell his birthright was reckless; he put the need of the moment above all other considerations. It's tempting to, like Esau, believe our desires must be satisfied right away. Such a frame of mind frequently leads to sin and unwelcome consequences.

Proverbs 16:26 says: "A worker's appetite works for him; his mouth urges him on." The desire to eat makes us get up in the morning and go to work. Our hunger pushes us forward; it's a good thing, part of God's plan for us. This is true even when the Lord makes us wait (as He often does).

Isn't this also true for the other things we want? I've discovered from experience that when God makes me wait, His answer is much better than what I could have obtained by rushing ahead of Him. Anticipating the good the Lord has for us motivates us to wait for it, or work for it in the way He desires.

Like Esau, we get in trouble when we run ahead of the Lord's provision and demand instant gratification of our longings. Sometimes He makes us wait a very long time while He is working out other situations in our lives, but in the end, we will find that He rewards our patience.

2. The Danger of Ignoring Eternity

In 1984, contemporary Christian artist Twila Paris wrote a song titled "Forever Eyes." The words to this song describe the perspective Esau lacked. The lyrics contrast living for the moment versus having eyes that see beyond the present and into eternity. The song emphasizes our need to look beyond what's right in front of us to matters that have eternal value.

Second Corinthians 4:17–18 says:

> For this light momentary affliction is preparing for us an eternal weight of glory beyond all comparison, as we look not to the

things that are seen but to the things that are unseen. For the things that are seen are transient, but the things that are unseen are eternal.

Esau epitomizes those who live with a one-world perspective. The great promises God made to his grandfather, Abraham, represented something in the distant future with no real worth at the moment. Esau valued fleeting realities over eternal values that we can't see. As a result, despite his later acquisition of great wealth and power, we regard him as a failure, one deemed "godless" by the writer of Hebrews.

Scripture doesn't indicate what Abraham taught his descendants about eternity or the future resurrection. However, we read in Hebrews 11:13–19 that the patriarch believed in God's ability to raise the dead, and he looked forward to a "city" beyond this life. He walked in faith regarding the New Jerusalem the Apostle John would describe much later (see Revelation chapters 21–22).

Abraham possessed an eternal perspective; he saw far beyond his current circumstances. Hebrews 11:16 says he desired "a better country, a heavenly one." We can safely assume he passed this vision of the future, of eternity, on to Isaac and possibly to Jacob and Esau as well, who would have been teenagers when Abraham died.

Throughout the New Testament, the apostles point believers to our "blessed hope" of the return of Jesus for His Church (see Titus 2:11–13). At the end of the book of Revelation, we also have a wondrous promise of a glorious eternity in which there will be no more suffering, death, or tears (Revelation 21:4).

As we face inevitable challenges, we must never lose sight of the thrilling hope that begins with Jesus' appearing. That's when He will take us to the place He is preparing for us (John 14:2–3). That is the substance of the "blessed hope" of the Gospel!

In such a time as this, we must not lose sight of eternity and the imminent appearing of Jesus. He is surely coming for us soon!

In far too many Bible-believing churches, sermons reverberate a theme of gaining "your best life now." This simply isn't a statement based on biblical truth. Believers today need an eternal perspective more than ever before!

3. The Danger of Gathering Wealth Without Regard for The Lord

When Jacob and Esau reconciled, Esau's gracious attitude toward his brother likely might have resulted from the riches and fame he had gained in the intervening years. During the twenty years the siblings were apart, Esau obtained all the material blessings, power, and attention he could ever desire. He approached Jacob with four hundred men—a sign of considerable wealth and great worldly influence (Genesis 32:6).

I believe Esau, as his wealth increased, forgot about the stolen blessing. He had all he wanted from this life, and that was enough; what did he really miss by not receiving his father's blessing? We see no sign of reverence for the Lord in Esau's life or in the lives of his descendants.

Esau brings to mind the Lord's parable about the rich fool in Luke 12:16–21. At the end of a bountiful harvest, the rich man vainly reflected on his wealth. Thinking his affluence came as the result of his own efforts, he boasted about his vast fortune and financial security.

For thirty-five years, I lived in Iowa, where, during autumn I often saw massive harvesters in the field loading corn into large trailers pulled by semi-trucks. Putting Jesus' parable in modern terms, I imagine a farmer feeling quite satisfied with his bountiful harvest as he watches truckload after truckload of grain going out for sale or as the bins on his farm fill up with grain to feed his cattle for the years to come.

The foolish farmer in Luke's account overlooked the Lord's role in providing the harvest and failed to thank Him for it. He focused solely on his own efforts to secure his future. He did not consider eternity or the lost state of his soul.

Death came that very night for the farmer in Jesus' story. For Esau, the end did not come quickly, yet the result was the same. He later died, and his great wealth and power vanished like a vapor. The question Jesus asked in Mark 8:36 seems pertinent in Esau's case: "What does it profit a man to gain the whole world and forfeit his soul?" I wonder if Jesus was thinking about Esau when He posed that question.

From a worldly perspective, Esau was anything but a failure. In addition to his success in acquiring livestock, riches, and great power, his descendants became the ancient nation of Edom. What did he lose from an earthly perspective by failing to obtain his father's blessing?

Jacob became the father of Israel, and Esau became the forefather of Edom. One might look at this from a human perspective and say they both enjoyed earthly success. Of course, this overlooks the fact that the Messiah would come through Jacob and his son, Judah.

God's Word views the two brothers quite differently. The writer of Hebrews praises the faith of Jacob (Hebrews 11:21), but says Esau was "godless" (Hebrews 12:16). Jacob's name appears in the "hall of fame" for his faith while Scripture emphasizes the futility and worthlessness of Esau's life.

Which evaluation would you prefer at the close of your life?

The nation of Edom no longer exists. Like its founder, it flourished for a while and then vanished from the pages of history.

The descendants of Jacob, however, remain, and they possess a glorious future. Israel now miraculously exists as a nation—and, during the Millennium, Jesus will rule the world from His seat upon the throne of David in the city of Jerusalem. God's not finished with Israel, Jacob's descendants; He will gloriously restore their Kingdom after Jesus' Second Coming.

Walking with God

What does Esau teach us about our walk with God? He demonstrates the danger of ignoring spiritual realities for the sake of temporary pleasures. Those who walk with the Lord recognize that the things of this life are fleeting, a vapor, while we will enjoy our inheritance in Heaven forever.

The Apostle Peter says we have been "born again to a living hope…
to an inheritance that is imperishable, undefiled, and unfading, kept in
heaven for [us], who by God's power are being guarded through faith
for a salvation ready to be revealed in the last time" (1 Peter 1:3–5).
The Lord doesn't redeem us so we can enjoy our "best life now." No! As
believers we have an eternal inheritance that cannot fade away. *We are
bound for glory.*

Peter later instructed us with these words: "Therefore, preparing
your minds for action, and being sober-minded, set your hope fully on
the grace that will be brought to you at the revelation of Jesus Christ"
(1 Peter 1:13). Our hope rests solely in Jesus and in His promises of
eternal life.

Romans 8:24 says "we were saved" in the hope of Jesus' appearing,
for it's at that time He will give us imperishable glorified bodies, and we
will experience our adoption into God's forever family (see also 1 Corinthians 15:50–55).

Many passages in the New Testament draw our attention to our glorious hope—the realization that this life is not all we have. Yet many of
us live as though this life *is* all we have. This erroneous perspective causes
us to miss the multitude of signs that tell us we're living in the last days.

Both Gehazi and Esau illustrate the danger of being materialistic,
coveting the things of this world for the sake of temporary pleasure. Esau
had great riches and Gehazi began as a poor servant of Elisha, yet both
became obsessed with possessions at the expense of what really matters.

STUDY GUIDE

Chapter 8

Esau: The Son Who Lived for the Moment

Passages: Genesis 25:19–35; 27:1–46
Key verses: Hebrews 12:16; 2 Corinthians 4:17–18; Luke 12:16–21

Questions for discussion:

1. What does the selling of his birthright tell us about Esau's character?

2. What did Isaac fail to consider when he decided to bless Esau?

3. Why might we suspect that Esau's anger at the stolen blessing was all about the temporary and monetary aspect rather than having anything to do with the long-term spiritual realities that came with it?

4. How does Esau's life demonstrate the folly of seeking immediate gratification for one's desires rather than waiting on the Lord?

5. How does Esau illustrate the danger of living with a one-world, temporal perspective?

6. What does Titus 2:11–13 reveal about the future hope we have in Christ? Why is it important to live with an eternal outlook?

7. How does the parable about the rich fool in Luke 12:16–21 relate to the life of Esau?

STUDY GUIDE

Chapter 8

8. What should be our proper perspective of the things of this world versus eternal realities? How does Esau's example warn us in this regard?
9. What is your key take-away from Esau's preoccupation with temporal gain rather than pursuing things that have eternal value attached to them?

Key lesson: Esau's life demonstrates the danger of ignoring eternal realities for the sake of temporary pleasures. Those who walk with the Lord recognize that the things of this life are fleeting, while our inheritance in Heaven will remain ours forever (see 1 Peter 1:3–5).

9

ELI

THE HIGH PRIEST WHO IDOLIZED HIS SONS

The fear of man lays a snare, but whoever trusts in the LORD is safe.

—PROVERBS 29:25

The most powerful people in the world wanted to kill him. However, they gave him one last chance to submit to their demands and agree with their traditions and doctrines. If he did that, all would be well. If not, they would murder him.

In 1521, the last vestiges of the Roman Empire, along with the Roman Catholic Church, convened the Diet of Worms. The title of this assembly had nothing to do with poor nutrition, but with the Catholic Church defending its long-held beliefs against a supposed heretic, one who dared to oppose the long-established practices and dogmas of the Church.

Johann Eck, acting as the spokesman for the Roman emperor, asked Martin Luther to denounce the errors in his writings once and for all. Luther, however, stood by his convictions and Scripture with his famous response:

Unless I am convinced by Scripture and plain reason—I do not accept the authority of popes and councils, for they have contradicted each other—my conscience is captive to the Word of God. I cannot and I will not recant anything, for to go against conscience is neither right nor safe. God help me. Amen.[11]

Another version of Luther's statement adds these words: "Here I stand, I cannot do otherwise."[12] Many believe they are genuine, but others attribute them to a later editing of his remarks. The words aptly summarize his sentiment, even if they're not authentic.

After making his bold pronouncement, Luther escaped the clutches of his adversaries. As the result of his courageous stance, his teachings on justification by faith forever changed the course of Church history. When faced with death, he stood up for the truths of God's Word.

It's easy to admire such bravery; we applaud those who take such a stand without fearing the consequences of what others might think of or do to them.

In our own lives, however, it's sometimes a different story. We feel the pressure to go along with the crowd, to not speak up when what we believe is at stake. We let the fear of others—or their opinions—dictate our behavior.

Eli, the next character in our study, exemplifies the danger of caring more about what others think of us than we do about obeying the Lord. He didn't strongly rebuke and punish his sons for their extreme wickedness. His weak response to their evil behavior brought God's judgment to him and his family.

Eli's Compromise

Eli served Israel as both high priest and judge in ancient Israel. When we first meet him in Scripture, he mistook Hannah's bitter weeping and silent prayer for a son as signs of drunkenness. When she explained that her behavior was because of the fervency of her prayer, Eli replied, "Go in peace, and the God of Israel grant your petition that you have made to him" (1 Samuel 1:17). His words gave Hannah confidence that God would grant her plea for a child.

God later honored Eli's words, as well as Hannah's faith, by giving her a son, whom she named Samuel. In keeping with the vow that she would give her son to the Lord, Hannah and her husband later left Samuel under Eli's care (1 Samuel 1:24–28).

Despite Eli's faithfulness to the Lord, he failed to stop the wickedness of his own sons (1 Samuel 2:12–17, 22–25). Through a prophet, the Lord pronounced judgment on Eli and his descendants, emphasizing the area of his greatest shortcoming:

> Why then do you scorn my sacrifices and my offerings that I commanded for my dwelling, and honor your sons above me by fattening yourselves on the choicest parts of every offering of my people Israel? (2 Samuel 2:29).

The priest pleased his sons, Hophni and Phinehas, rather than God; this led to great compromise in Eli's service to the Lord. While he never bowed to a wooden image, he made an idol of his sons' affection. They took a place in his life that should have belonged exclusively to the Lord. His misguided love for his sons caused him to take a weak stand regarding their great sins.

The Wickedness of Hophni and Phinehas

Scripture introduces Hophni and Phinehas as "worthless men" who "did not know the Lord" (2 Samuel 2:12). The Bible uses this same description of men who encouraged people to worship other gods (Deuteronomy 13:13); of Nabal, who was recklessly foolish (1 Samuel 25:17), and of the men who provided the false testimony that enabled Jezebel to put

Naboth to death (1 Kings 21:10). "Worthless men" points to Eli's sons' extreme wickedness and contempt for God and His ways.

What did they do to deserve such a harsh evaluation of their lives?

When the Israelites offered peace sacrifices to the Lord, the Law allowed a priest to take the breast and right thigh as food (Leviticus 7:34). The priest took his share *after* he had properly offered the meat to the Lord and *after* the priest had burned the fat upon the altar (Leviticus 7:31). In this way, God provided for the needs of those who served Him in the tabernacle and later in the Temple.

Furthermore, it was the custom for the priest to plunge his fork into the pot when the meat was boiling and take for himself whatever the utensil brought up out of the pot (1 Samuel 2:14). (Boiling was the method of cooking specified for the priest's portion of meat [see Numbers 6:19–20].)

Hophni and Phinehas disregarded God's Word and the revered customs of their time. They sent their servants to get their portion of the offering *before* they burned the fat portions (1 Samuel 2:15). If the worshippers intended to comply with God's Law, Eli's sons threatened to take the meat from them by force (1 Samuel 2:16). His sons not only disobeyed the requirements of the Law, but threatened violence against those who wanted to obey the Lord.

First Samuel 2:17 says: "This sin of the young men was very great in the sight of the Lord, for the men treated the offering of the Lord with contempt." Hophni and Phinehas took what God intended as a way to provide for their needs and distorted it to satisfy their gluttonous appetite. Eli's sons desired the choice portions for themselves before the fire burned away the fat.

Hophni and Phinehas further demonstrated their wickedness by committing acts of immorality with the women who served at the entrance to the tent of meeting (1 Samuel 2:22). They did not keep their great sin a secret; many people witnessed it and complained to Eli regarding his sons' behavior. Eli rebuked the young men for this, albeit mildly, but they refused to listen (1 Samuel 2:23–25).

The actions of Eli's sons displayed their total disdain for the Lord. They arrogantly attempted to satisfy their lusts while presuming to serve Him. As a result of their wickedness, the Lord wanted to kill the depraved priests (1 Samuel 2:25). He certainly couldn't let one of them become the high priest, which normally would be the case since they were the sons of the high priest at that time.

Eli's Response

Eli's response to the sins of his sons is at best puzzling. As high priest and judge, he had a double obligation to stop his sons' evil behavior. Instead, he joined in their abuses of the sacrificial meat and became quite overweight as a result.

Eli rebuked the young men for their adultery, but the mildness of his scolding did not match the seriousness of the offense; nor was it enough to make them change their ways. His reprimand was far too little, much too late.

When the Lord sent a "man of God" to warn Eli about the consequences of Hophni and Phinehas' sins, He included Eli in His judgment. He accused all of them of "fattening" themselves by taking for themselves the choicest portions of the offerings (1 Samuel 2:29).

Scripture later notes that Eli's obesity was a factor that contributed to his death (1 Samuel 4:18). Rather than correct the perversion of his sons, Eli joined in their gluttony and engaged in flagrant disregard for the Law.

Eli should have removed Hophni and Phinehas from their offices as priests and had them put to death for their adultery, which they didn't even attempt to hide. Eli's allegiance to his sons kept him from doing what was right in the eyes of the Lord, even after he knew about God's intention to administer judgment because of his sons' behavior. Could his enjoyment of the meat portions they stole from the worshippers and roasted for themselves have contributed to the emptiness of Eli's reprimand? It's entirely possible.

Proverbs 29:25 says, "The fear of man lays a snare, but whoever trusts in the Lord is safe." Eli's actions demonstrate how fearing others can become a trap leading to disastrous results. He feared his sons more than God, compelling His judgment to fall on Eli's entire family.

God's Judgment Falls

God's first revelation to Samuel showed how God honors those who don't give in to fearing others. Remarkably, the Lord repeated His sentence of judgment on Eli through young Samuel:

> For I told him that I would judge his family forever because of the sins he knew about; his sons made themselves contemptible, and he failed to restrain them. (1 Samuel 3:13, NIV; see also 1 Samuel 3:11–14)

Notice again the Lord's reference to Eli's failure to restrain his sons.

With coaxing from Eli, Samuel repeated God's words of judgment on the aging priest. Imagine having to deliver such a message to the one who has been raising you as your father. Although he might have feared Eli's response, Samuel faithfully told Eli all the Lord had revealed to him the previous night (1 Samuel 3:15–21).

Later, God's judgment fell on Eli and his family, just as the Lord had said. Faced with the prospect of defeat, the leaders of Israel decided to take the Ark of the Covenant into battle with them (1 Samuel 4:2–9). Displaying superstition rather than genuine faith in the Lord, they believed such action would ensure a victory over their enemy. It didn't.

Not only did the Philistines overcome the forces of Israel, but they also captured the Ark and killed both Hophni and Phineas. When Eli heard the enemy forces had seized the Ark, he fell off his chair, broke his neck, and died (1 Samuel 4:10–18).

It's significant that Eli fell to his death upon hearing the fate of the

Ark of the Covenant rather than when he learned of his sons' deaths. Because of God's warnings, Eli may have expected God's judgment to fall on Hophni and Phineas. He did not, however, anticipate that the Philistines would capture the most sacred furnishing of the tabernacle.

The fact that he fell to his death at that instant speaks to Eli's faith. The news of what happened to the Ark of the Covenant caused him the most grief and demonstrated his ongoing devotion to the Lord despite his serious failures with sons.

Courage to Take a Strong Stand

While we might be quick to judge Eli for honoring his sons above the Lord, don't we find ourselves at times seeking to impress others? I recognize this tendency in my own life. The words of Proverbs 29:25 have more than once convicted me of my sin as I've recognized occasions when I have replaced my reverence for God with a fear of others.

It's certainly not wrong to care about others' opinions. Problems arise, however, when we follow Eli's example and make idols of those opinions.

I admire the courage of Martin Luther, who chose to remain true to the Lord and His Word even when he faced almost-certain death. But why is it so hard for us to follow Luther's example versus that of Eli?

What considerations might help us in this matter?

1. Play to an Audience of One.

During my college years and for many years afterward, I played trombone solos in the churches I attended and served at as pastor. In doing so, I often felt a tension between glorifying the Lord versus seeking to impress others. Was the addition of a few difficult notes necessary, or was it simply to show off my skills? At times, I admit, my motive was a mixture of the two.

I later heard a phrase that might have helped me as I prepared for these solos. It speaks to doing all that we do for an "audience of One." Whenever we exercise the talents God gives us, we must always remember we are playing to an "audience of One." It's what pleases the Lord that matters, not what may or may not please others.

The Apostle Paul addressed this in 1 Thessalonians 2:4: "So we speak, not to please man, but to please God who tests our hearts." The apostle also recognized the conflict between honoring God and impressing people. He deeply cared for the Thessalonian believers and made every effort to make sure nothing about his behavior interfered with his messages to them. However, he never compromised the truth of the Gospel. Such a balance pleased the Lord then—and it still does.

Paul later asked the believers in Thessalonica to follow his example of trying to "please God" in all things (1 Thessalonians 4:1). Paul modeled this through his willingness to tenderly care for the Thessalonians while at the same time faithfully proclaiming the whole truth of the Gospel.

In the end, it's what we do for the Lord that counts. Those are the works that will endure when tested with fire on the day we stand before the Lord as holy and blameless saints (1 Corinthians 3:11–15). The Lord sees all our motives and knows whether we are truly serving Him or merely attempting to impress others.

It helps me to recognize that the Lord's opinion is above all other considerations. What good is it if I impress everyone around me, but not the Lord, with my service? Conversely, if God is truly pleased with my devotion to Him, does it really mean much what others think?

It's not an issue of ignoring the opinions of others or rejecting valid criticism, but of doing all for God's glory.

2. Seek Spiritual Results.

When asked to teach a large Sunday school class of singles in my church several years ago, I decided to talk about Saul and waiting on the Lord (the material covered in chapter 1). One week before I was to speak,

I hurt my back playing tennis. X–rays revealed advanced degenerative arthritis in my back, and my doctor prescribed extended physical therapy, which later brought needed relief to my chronic condition. He also gave me pills to take—a new medicine designed to help ease severe arthritis pain.

Looking back, I wonder why I didn't postpone teaching that class. Everyone would have understood, but I plunged ahead in spite of the pain. Perhaps I thought the new medication would bring relief to the soreness and muscle spasms before I stood in front of the class. It didn't.

As I taught that morning, I remained ever mindful of the pain in my back as well as the stiff and awkward movements it caused. The medication caused my mouth to become extremely dry, more so than with any other I had ever taken. I started the class with full glasses of water and orange juice, and needed to request refills for both at least once while speaking.

As I finished, I thought it must have been my worst attempt ever at teaching. I wanted to run away and hide. It seemed like a disaster! I felt as though I should apologize.

The response of the class, however, surprised and overwhelmed me; it's something I will never forget. In spite of my distracting pain and continual dry mouth, the Holy Spirit worked through me that morning.

Afterward, many of the class members told me the Lord had spoken to their hearts as I taught. One person asked if I had a tape of the lesson. Six weeks later, another thanked me and reminded me again of how the Lord had used my words that morning to encourage her. I had never before received such a positive and ongoing response to my teaching or preaching.

The Lord taught me a valuable lesson that day. He is the One who uses my words, whether it's through speaking or writing, for His purposes and ultimately for His glory. It's never my ability that impacts the lives of others, but rather the Holy Spirit working through me (or most certainly in spite of me, as was the case that morning so long ago).

God takes what we offer Him and uses it for His glory, even when we think we've failed. On the other hand, sometimes we may believe we've done an amazing job, yet we don't impact others in any meaningful way.

When I was in college, a man who came to speak at one of our regular chapel services did an excellent job of teaching God's Word, explaining the various usages of Greek words in the text and telling interesting and relevant stories. However, afterward, I couldn't remember anything of significance he had said. Others told me they felt the same emptiness after hearing him speak. Despite his highly impressive delivery and great story-telling ability, the Spirit didn't appear to be working through him on that day.

We must trust God alone as we minister to others. He uses our gifts, whether it's teaching, giving, helping, leading, encouraging others, or even reproving others for their sins. Only the Lord can take what we offer and use it to bring about change in the lives of those around us. If we remember this, we will be less tempted to fear how others might respond.

This doesn't at all mean we shouldn't strive for excellence in whatever we do for God. He is honored when we try our best. Proverbs 21:31 properly sums up the balance between efforts and results: "The horse is made ready for the day of battle, but the victory belongs to the Lord."

Wanting to yield spiritual results does not imply that we shouldn't prepare or put forth our very best effort, not at all. Once we've done so, however, we must depend on the Lord for any spiritual blessings that might flow into the lives of others.

3. Rest in God's Total and Unending Acceptance.

As high priest, Eli went into the Holy of Holies once a year, on the Day of Atonement. There, he sprinkled blood on the mercy seat, asking for God's forgiveness on behalf of the people of Israel. Year after year, he experienced the Lord's mercy toward himself and Israel on the basis of a sacrifice that looked forward to Jesus' death on the cross.

Eli, however, never adequately applied God's acceptance to his personal life. Instead, he sought the approval of his sons. So often, fear of people springs from a failure to appreciate and contemplate the never-ending approval we already have from our heavenly Father.

Despite knowing everything bad about us, the Lord loves us, wants our friendship, spends every moment of every day thinking about what's best for us, and eagerly waits for us to spend time with Him. God's grace and mercy enable us to stand in His presence forever free from all condemnation (Romans 8:1, 31-39).

The more we bask in the Lord's surpassing and unending love, the less we'll need to look to others to fill that desire. If the Creator of the universe loves us, what does it matter if people reject us? I remind myself often of this truth, especially when I experience the rejection of others.

Of course, there are times when we need to listen to and consider the criticism from others. However, we must not allow their opinions to usurp our devotion to God. Recognizing His total and unconditional acceptance of us as His children certainly deters our tendency to make an idol of others' approval.

Walking with God

Eli's example highlights the danger of becoming preoccupied with the opinions of others, of honoring people above the Lord. It's not that we should ignore what others think; problems arise, however, when our desire to please people trumps our devotion to the Lord, even when our own children challenge us to compromise our beliefs, as is often the case during these perilous times.

The One who created everything we see loves us unconditionally and constantly seeks our eternal well-being. Understanding this deflates our dependence upon the approval of others. If the Creator of the universe loves me so completely, why am I so prone to rely on others' opinions?

Our purpose in whatever we do for the Lord must not be to impress

others, but to allow the Holy Spirit to work through our gifts and talents
to accomplish the results He desires. Sometimes that means we must
take a strong stand for the Lord and His Word.

This doesn't mean we should fail to strive for excellence in serving
Him and look for ways to improve our abilities in the areas where He
has gifted us. It's just that, as we strive to do the best job possible, we
must remember that only the Holy Spirit produces lasting results in
those we serve with our gifts.

STUDY GUIDE

Chapter 9

Eli: The High Priest Who Idolized His Sons

Passages: 1 Samuel 1:9–28; 2:12–36; 4:12–22
Key verses: Proverbs 29:25; 1 Thessalonians 2:4

Questions for discussion:

1. What positive aspects of Eli's life do we see from reading 1 Samuel 1:9–28?

2. How does Scripture describe Hophni and Phinehas? What behavior caused the Lord to want to kill them?

3. What evidence do we have that Eli also partook of the meat that his sons acquired by breaking the laws about sacrifices?

4. Why did Eli have a "double obligation" to deal forcibly with the wickedness of his two sons?

5. What news caused Eli to fall to his death? Why is that so significant?

6. What does it mean to play to an "audience of One?"

7. How does desiring spiritual results in our ministries steer us away from serving only for the approval of others?

8. Whose acceptance should matter the most to us, and why does it matter so much?

9. In what areas do you struggle with seeking the approval of those around you?

STUDY GUIDE

Chapter 9

Key lesson: Eli's example shows us the danger of becoming preoccupied with the opinions of others, of honoring people above the Lord. It's not that we should ignore what others think; problems arise, however, when our desire to please people trumps our devotion to the Lord.

10

DIOTREPHES

THE CHURCH LEADER WHO EXALTED HIMSELF

*Jesus called them to him and said to them, "You know that those
who are considered rulers of the Gentiles lord it over them, and
their great ones exercise authority over them. But it shall not be
so among you. But whoever would be great among you must be
your servant."*

—MARK 10:42–43

In 2012, a fascinating miniseries debuted on the History Channel. *The
Men Who Built America* chronicled the business empires of Cornelius
Vanderbilt, John D. Rockefeller, Andrew Carnegie, J. P. Morgan, and
Henry Ford. The weekly dramas featured their accomplishments as well
as the fierce competition between them as they battled for both money
and power.

I loved the episodes because they provided a fresh look at history; I
learned a lot through the dramatization of past events. America benefited
from the innovations implemented by these men, who brought such
things as electricity into all our homes and made automobiles affordable
to everyone rather than just the wealthy.

However, the series also revealed a dark side of these business titans. In one way or another, they destroyed the lives of business leaders who got in their way. Their profit motive led to abusing workers in their factories. Men worked long hours under extremely dangerous conditions in Carnegie's steel mills. Exhaustion and extreme heat made their work perilous and caused numerous deaths.

Such aspiration for power and prestige also causes considerable damage in our churches. Jesus taught His disciples that leadership in the church must be vastly different from how it's exercised in the world, where leaders frequently rule by imposing their will on those beneath them.

Diotrephes followed the world's pattern of leadership; he sought to rule over his church rather than to serve those under his care. His desire for control led the Apostle John to write a short epistle concerning his abuse of authority; in it, the apostle rebuked Diotrephes for not only failing to provide hospitality, but also for his treatment of those in his church who sought to be hospitable toward travelers who shared their beliefs (3 John).

Gaius' Example

John addressed his third epistle to Gaius rather than to Diotrephes (3 John 1). Previously, Diotrephes had spurned John's authority in regard to a letter the aged apostle sent to him (3 John 9). He may have done this by refusing to read it to the believers under his care. In order to get the attention of the wayward leader, John followed up with this letter, 3 John, addressed to Gaius, who—in contrast to Diotrephes—delighted to welcome strangers into his home.

John did not specify whether Gaius was another leader in the same church as Diotrephes or if he ministered in a nearby town. The manner in which the apostle mentioned the issue regarding Diotrephes, however, suggests that while Gaius knew Diotrephes, he wasn't aware of the problems Diotrephes was causing where he served.

John wrote as though he was informing Gaius of the matter, which indicates Gaius probably ministered elsewhere. If he served in the same city, it's certain he would have been aware of the issues caused by Diotrephes since they affected so many people.

The apostle commended Gaius for his hospitality to travelers who came his way (3 John 5–8). At the church where John served at the time, which may have been in Ephesus, fellow believers praised Gaius for his help in providing for their needs while they stayed with him. They clearly felt blessed by the lodging Gaius and other congregants gave them as they traveled through his city.

During this time in the late first century AD, missionaries and teachers journeyed throughout the Roman Empire preaching the Gospel to the lost and building up believers in other communities. As you might imagine, travel at the time wasn't as easy as it is today when we have numerous hotels and restaurants. Early Christian travelers depended on the warm reception of fellow believers as they journeyed from town to town throughout the empire.

Gaius exemplified what the writer of Hebrews admired: "Let brotherly love continue. Do not neglect to show hospitality to strangers, for thereby some have entertained angels unawares" (Hebrews 13:1–2). This certainly motivated Christians to invite strangers into their homes. Doing so, they might provide accommodations for angels posing as itinerant teachers.

Diotrephes' Character

Diotrephes not only didn't show kindness to early Christian travelers, but he also went as far as to prevent others in his church from providing the travelers with lodging. What would make him behave this way? Let's first look at his character, for this is where John began addressing the problems Diotrephes caused.

The name "Diotrephes" means "one nourished by Jupiter." This identifies him as a Gentile convert to Christianity, as no Jew would give the name of a pagan god to their child. Furthermore, based on John's description, Diotrephes was a leader or pastor in his church and exercised considerable influence over those who attended.

The apostle characterized the pastor as someone "who likes to put himself first," a person who loves to have preeminence over others (3 John 9). Diotrephes enjoyed being in a position where he could dictate the behavior of others. As we will see, problems arose because he valued his authority over serving others in the Body of Christ.

This desire to be in charge led Diotrephes to reject John's apostolic authority. As mentioned earlier, the apostle had earlier written a letter to Diotrophes' church that the pastor did not acknowledge. We can assume the letter addressed the need for him to lead his flock by displaying hospitality to others.

It's difficult to imagine someone disregarding a letter from a living apostle who had walked with Jesus, witnessed His resurrection, and experienced the Holy Spirit's arrival at Pentecost. Yet that is exactly what Diotrephes did. It's likely that he destroyed the letter from the apostle, which is unthinkable from our perspective.

John complained that Diotrephes was "talking wicked nonsense against us" (3 John 10). How could a leader in the early church, one who personally knew John, the beloved disciple, openly slander him? Yet, in his arrogance, Diotrephes not only rebelled against John's authority, but maliciously maligned him in front of fellow believers. What could have caused him to show such disdain for John?

Diotrephes may have grown tired of John's interference, wanting to run his church in his own way. Or did he resist the apostle's influence based on their age difference? John was at least ninety years old by this time, and we can safely assume Diotrephes was much younger. Whatever the cause, Diotrephes thought he could run things just fine without the intervention of the much-older man.

Diotrephes' love of preeminence stands in direct contradiction not only to Christ's instructions, but also to His example. Regarding our

Savior's humility and our need to imitate it, Paul said, "Have this mind among yourselves, which is yours in Christ Jesus, who, though he was in the form of God, did not count equality with God a thing to be grasped, but emptied himself, by taking the form of a servant, being born in the likeness of men" (Philippians 2:5–7).

Rather than follow Jesus' pattern of service, Diotrephes exalted himself at the expense of others. He resembled the power-seekers in *The Men Who Built America* more than he did the Savior.

John didn't criticize Diotrephes for doctrinal error; the apostle didn't have an issue with what Diotrephes taught. Rather, the apostle found fault with his unwillingness to display love for fellow believers. Motivated by pride, the young leader sought to demonstrate that he was in control, even to the point of rebuffing John's authority as an apostle and spreading malicious gossip about him.

Diotrephes' Behavior

Diotrephes refused hospitality to fellow ministers of the Word as they traveled through his area (3 John 10). As a leader in his church, he should have set the example by welcoming strangers into his home, as Gaius had done. Instead, he declined to welcome them and even hindered those under him from doing so.

To make matters worse, Diotrephes excommunicated those who went against his wishes by providing lodging for traveling evangelists and teachers. Unlike today, those put out of his church didn't have the luxury of going to another place of worship down the road or in a nearby city. There were no other options for Christian fellowship and teaching for those put out of a body of believers at that time.

It's no wonder that John, known as the Apostle of Love, spoke in such harsh tones regarding Diotrephes. John was not only defending his authority as an apostle of Jesus, but he was also seeking to stop Diotrephes' abusive display of power over those under his care.

While hospitality remains an important ministry today, it's not as critical—in a practical sense—as it was during the early years of the church. However, although the issues have changed, leaders with Diotrephes' mentality often rise to places of authority in our churches. That's why the message of 3 John is so vital today, more so than ever before.

Serving Others in Humility

When people like Diotrephes become leaders in our churches, their love for themselves causes great harm in the Body of Christ. Whether the matter involved is hospitality, the songs chosen for worship, or the color of drapes in the library, it's important to remember the Lord's example of humility in leadership.

Those who follow Gaius' example bring beauty to the Body of Christ through their humble service to others, while those like Diotrephes harm fellow believers. This is why I believe the often-overlooked message contained in 3 John has so much value today.

From my recent experience in dealing with pastors who lead Bible-believing churches, many more often than not resemble Diotrophes. Humility is indeed a rare trait among pastors and laypeople alike today.

What can we learn from 3 John that will help us serve others with greater humility?

1. Recognize the Strength of Humility.

Several years ago, my wife and I visited Washington, DC. One of the highlights of our trip was seeing the Lincoln Memorial. Looking up at the giant statute of Abraham Lincoln seated on a huge marble chair, we might never imagine he was the humblest president in our nation's history.

Upon winning his first election as president, he appointed his chief rivals for the Republican nomination, William Henry Seward and

Salmon P. Chase, to key positions in his cabinet. Rather than punish them for their previous opposition to him, he rewarded them with choice posts in his administration. Lincoln described his reason for doing this as follows: "I had looked the party over and concluded that these were the very strongest men. Then I had no right to deprive the country of their service."[13]

In an article in *Psychology Today*, writer Russel Razzaque commented insightfully about Lincoln: "He put his own ego aside to appoint whoever he thought was best for the country, whenever a post needed to be filled."[14] Lincoln even named one of his harshest critics, Edwin Stanton, Secretary of War because he believed Stanton was the best person for the job. Never mind that, at one time, Stanton had described Lincoln as a "long-armed ape."[15] Can you imagine a president today giving a prestigious position to someone who had referred to him in such a way? I can't.

So, humility marked Lincoln's presidency. Putting aside his ego, however, did not diminish the quality of his leadership or authority during a perilous time in our country's history; instead, to this day, we honor him as one of our greatest presidents. His meekness neither kept him from making tough decisions nor weakened his leadership skills. On the contrary, it earned him more respect from others and enhanced the strength of his influence when our country needed it the most.

Likewise, cultivating a humble spirit doesn't mean we should fail to lead or exercise authority. In confronting Diotrephes about his sin, John showed us that humble leaders must at times also confront hurtful and sinful behavior when necessary. *Humility defines how we must lead; it's never an excuse for our failure to do so.*

Jesus prescribed humility for members of His Church in Mark 10:42–43:

> You know that those who are considered rulers of the Gentiles lord it over them, and their great ones exercise authority over them. But it shall not be so among you. But whoever would be great among you must be your servant.

The Lord knew Gentile, or worldly, leaders typically ruled solely to satisfy their own thirst for power, regardless of the wishes of those under them.

In the above passage, Jesus was responding to James and John's request to occupy places of power in Jesus' earthly kingdom (Mark 10:35–37). With this appeal, not only were they getting ahead of themselves in their expectation of Jesus' future Millennial Kingdom, but they were also displaying a worldly desire for authority. In response, Jesus told them their humble service, rather than their power to direct the lives of others, would signify their greatness.

In the example Jesus set for us, we see that His humility did not prevent Him from making bold statements and taking strong actions when needed. For example, He spoke sternly to the scribes and Pharisees at times. His gentleness in caring for the needs of others amplified the effectiveness of His firm and unyielding messages when He gave them, particularly for those who were leading His people astray with their legalism.

2. Recognize Authority.

In his book *Eye of the Storm*, Max Lucado recounts an oft-repeated story taken from the *U.S. Naval Institute Proceedings* magazine. The incident happened after two battleships had been on training maneuvers for several days. One foggy night when the visibility was quite poor, a lookout on one of the ships spotted a light in the distance and reported it to his captain. The captain issued a command to the other ship to change its course in order to avoid a collision.

The ship's commander received a response stating that *he* was the one who needed to change course. Sensing defiance to his authority, the captain sent a message back stressing his rank and position as the commander of a battleship. How dare anyone challenge him? While the captain far outranked the one refusing to comply with his command, he promptly changed course after receiving one final message in reply: "I'm a lighthouse."[16]

Regardless of how or where we serve the Lord, it's important to recognize His ultimate sovereignty over us and His Church. The most striking aspect of Diotrephes' behavior was his brutal disregard for John's calling as an apostle of the Lord. He went as far as to personally slander him in front of his church. Wow!

For us, John's authority seems unquestionable. He's like the lighthouse in the story Lucado recounted. If we find ourselves on a collision course with his words, or with any of the words of Scripture, we need to change course. The New Testament represents the teaching of the apostles in written form.

When we recognize and submit to those whom the Lord places over us, we display humility, which furthers the work of Christ. Whether we do so in regard to Scripture or to those God places above us, it always benefits those we serve when we submit. In 1 Thessalonians 5:12, Paul instructed us "to respect those who labor among you and are over you in the Lord." The apostle then concluded his remarks with, "Be at peace among yourselves" (1 Thessalonians 5:13).

As is so often the case, when respect for others is nonexistent in the church, peace is also absent. When people follow Diotrephes' example, regardless of their place in the Body of Christ, strife and divisions follow. This doesn't mean we may never disagree with those in leadership or they will never behave like Diotrephes. However, as we work through matters of conflict, we must not abandon respect for others.

Both regard for others and submission to those in authority have strong negative connotations in today's culture. Jesus, however, elevated the necessity of submission in all our relationships. In the Upper Room on the night before His crucifixion, Jesus spoke of His role in respect to the Father: "The words that I say to you I do not speak on my own authority, but the Father who dwells in me does his works" (John 14:10). Jesus willingly submitted to the will of His Father in Heaven; He followed the instruction of his Father in all that He did.

At times, doctrinal error makes it necessary to stand up for the truth of God's Word. I've found that those who interpret the words of Scripture based on human wisdom more often than not resemble the character of Diotrophes. Not only do they exhibit pride, but they resist the authority of God's Word.

3. Consider Your Influence on Others.

The behavior of those who hurt fellow believers, as did Diotrephes, damages the testimonies of those within the church. Imagine yourself as a neighbor of a family Diotrephes put out of the church because they showed hospitality to fellow believers. Do you think they would be eager to respond to the Gospel after seeing their neighbors treated in such a shameful way?

I am passionate about what I believe, especially in regard to the authority of God's Words and unfulfilled biblical prophecy. As such, it's easy for me to overlook harmony in my efforts to prove my point. I often forget Paul's admonition in 2 Timothy 2:24–25 that a teacher should not be "quarrelsome," but should correct others "with gentleness." While it is good to express strong feelings about what we believe to be true based on God's Word, we also risk harming the power of our influence on others when we neglect Paul's teaching in this passage and argue our case without showing respect.

Diotrephes' example brings me back to reality. I've seen the damage to churches (and thereby to their effectiveness in sharing the Gospel in their community) by those who proudly pursue their own interests at the expense of those around them. That's why it is essential to never forget the power of our example, always making sure our words humbly reflect the grace we ourselves enjoy, especially when dealing with those who disagree with or even oppose our efforts.

There is a time to show strength. As we see in Jesus' example, and even in President Lincoln's, humility and grace do not diminish the impact of our influence when we take a strong stand; on the contrary, they enhance it.

However, we must always remember Paul's instructions to correct others gently and with humility. When those who don't follow Christ witness a power struggle that tears apart a church, they're likely to conclude that believers are no different from themselves. Worse yet, they lose any desire to pursue a relationship with our Savior.

Walking with God

What does Diotrephes teach us about our walk with God? He illustrates the danger of serving the Lord in order to benefit ourselves rather than others.

During my time as a pastor, I saw firsthand the importance of godly, mature leadership, the kind Gaius exhibited. Chuck, a leader in the first church I pastored, used his position to serve others. His humility, coupled with godliness, gave him a strong voice not only in the church, but also out in the community. Because of that dynamic pairing of characteristics—humility and godliness—people in the city frequently requested his leadership services.

The Body of Christ sorely needs leaders like Gaius who follow the Savior's example and walk in the Spirit, allowing them to produce His fruit in their lives.

On the other hand, I have seen some pastors behave like Diotrephes. They all too eagerly dismiss the opinions of those they serve, especially if those disagreeing with them are much older. Like the picture we have of Diotrephes destroying the letter from the Apostle John, they proudly disregard the wisdom others offer and, at times, they even dismiss them from their churches.

STUDY GUIDE

Chapter 10

Diotrephes: The Church Leader Who Exalted Himself

Passage: 3 John

Key verses: Hebrews 13:1–2; Mark 10:42–45; 2 Timothy 2:24–25

Questions for discussion:

1. What issue led to John writing the epistle recorded in 3 John?
2. Why did the apostle send the letter to Gaius rather than to Diotrephes, who was the one causing the problems?
3. Why was hospitality especially important in the first-century AD church?
4. What commendations did John give Gaius?
5. What can we learn about the character of Diotrephes from reading 3 John?
6. Why was Diotrephes' behavior so destructive to the Body of Christ?
7. What does the example of Abraham Lincoln teach us about serving with humility?
8. What's so remarkable about Diotrephes' contempt of the Apostle John?
9. How did Diotrephes compromise the effectiveness of the church in the area where he served?

STUDY GUIDE

Chapter 10

10. Has pride ever caused you to display a lack of respect toward those in authority in the church? What was the result?

Key lesson: Diotrephes illustrates the danger of serving the Lord in order to benefit ourselves rather than others. Conversely, the church sorely needs leaders like Gaius who follow the Savior's example and walk in the Spirit, allowing them to produce His fruit in their lives.

11

ASA

THE KING WHO STARTED FAST, FINISHED LAST

For the eyes of the LORD run to and fro throughout the whole earth, to give strong support to those whose heart is blameless toward him.

—2 CHRONICLES 16:9

Although I'm not a fan of horse racing, I enjoy watching the Triple Crown races each spring, especially if a horse has a chance to win all three races. One thing I've observed is that the horse who gets out to an early lead rarely wins the race. More often than not, the winning horse comes from behind to claim the prize.

This happened in the 2017 running of the Preakness Stakes, the second race in the Triple Crown. Most people expected Always Dreaming, the winner of the Kentucky Derby and the heavy favorite, to win this race as well. As anticipated, he jumped out to an early lead and kept that position for almost the entire race before the unexpected happened—he began to fade. A horse named Cloud Computing came from behind to win while Always Dreaming finished in a disappointing eighth place.

The performance of Asa, the next character in our study, resembles that of Always Dreaming in that 2017 event. For much of his life, Asa remained close to the Lord, following in His ways as well as in those of King David. However, he surprisingly drifted far away from God later in his life. Because of the king's robust faithfulness to the Lord right out of the gate—in the early years of his reign—it's a struggle to understand how he could abandon the Lord so completely in his later years, as he approached the finish line.

I've often heard it said that the "Christian life resembles a marathon much more than a sprint." Like Asa, it's possible to begin our relationship with the Lord like fast runners cruising along just fine...until trouble arises. As our pace slows, we're tempted to give up, stop running. We soon find ourselves behind where we once were in terms of living by faith and serving the Lord.

What can we learn from Asa's example that will help us finish strong in our walk with the Savior and endure to the end of the race before us? Let's start by reviewing the highlights of the king's reign.

A Fantastic Start

Asa began his reign as king of Judah in a manner worthy of King David. Both the writers of 1 Kings and 2 Chronicles praised his initial faithfulness to the Lord. One of his first acts as king was to remove his grandmother, Maacah, as the queen mother because of her idolatry and pagan influence on the nation. He destroyed the "abominable image" of Asherah she had set up and worshipped (1 Kings 15:11–13). He also put an end to all the decadent sexual practices associated with the worship of this god.

The opening years of Asa's forty-one-year reign were peaceful. As he fortified the cities of Judah, he gave all the credit to God: "The land is still ours, because we have sought the LORD our God. We have sought him, and he has given us peace on every side" (2 Chronicles 14:7). These words not only reveal his trust in God, but also an understanding of the blessings and warnings Moses wrote about in Deuteronomy 27–28. The king recognized God as Israel's source of security, and he realized that security stemmed from the nation's continued faithfulness to the Lord.

Asa's first significant test came in the form of an invasion led by Zerah the Ethiopian. Zerah's one million soldiers dwarfed the combined forces of Judah and Benjamin (2 Chronicles 14:8–9). As Asa led his men out to meet this challenge, he realized that only the Lord could deliver them from such an ominous threat.

His prayer revealed the strength of his faith:

> O LORD, there is none like you to help, between the mighty and the weak. Help us, O LORD our God, for we rely on you, and in your name we have come against this multitude. O LORD, you are our God; let not man prevail against you. (2 Chronicles 14:11)

Asa understood his great disadvantage and cried out to the Lord for help. He asked for a great victory and placed his confidence in Israel's God. Like Jonathan, Saul's son, Asa saw the battle as being waged between God and His enemies, so the king looked to the Lord to do great things.

The Lord answered the king's prayer in a mighty way. Second Chronicles 14:12 simply states the facts of the ensuing victory: "So the LORD defeated the Ethiopians before Asa and before Judah, and the Ethiopians fled." Despite overwhelming odds against Judah, the Lord responded to the king's prayer and defeated the invading army that vastly outnumbered that of Judah.

After the great victory, God sent a prophet, Azariah, to Asa with both a promise and a warning. The prophet assured the king that the Lord was with him and would continue to reward the king's faith. As an indicator of things to come, the prophet cautioned that if Asa turned away from the Lord, He would likewise "forsake" Asa (2 Chronicles 15:1–7). At this point in his reign, Asa resembled the favored racehorse, Always Dreaming; he appeared out front leading his nation in a God-honoring way.

Removing idolatry and gaining victory over the imposing enemy prompted a great revival in Judah. Asa's faithfulness to the Lord inspired not only the Southern Kingdom of Israel, but the entire nation as well. Many from the Northern Kingdom of Israel went to Jerusalem to worship the Lord after they saw that God's presence was truly with Asa (2 Chronicles 15:8–15). They came with a longing to serve the Lord.

Judging by the sacrifices, worship, and rejoicing throughout Judah, it would be logical to think Asa would never turn away from the Lord. It did seem so, for a time. In fact, his kingdom remained peaceful until the thirty-sixth year of his reign, when he faced another test of faith.

Asa Forgets

When the Lord saw the king beginning to rely on his own strength, He interrupted the lengthy calm period the nation had been enjoying with a test. It began when Baasha, the king of Israel, fortified the city of Ramah, which was just five miles north of Jerusalem. By revitalizing this city, Baasha prevented access to Jerusalem along a main trade route. Blocking entry to the city of David also made it difficult for people in the north to worship the Lord at the Temple there (2 Chronicles 16:1). King Baasha saw their trips to Jerusalem as possibly jeopardizing his rule.

Years earlier, when he had faced the threat from the Ethiopians, Asa had called out to the Lord for help. This time, however, he took silver and gold from the Temple and his palace, and used the kingdom's treasures to buy the help of Ben-hadad, the king of Syria. Along with the payment, Asa asked the Syrian king to break his covenant with Baasha and instead attack the Northern Kingdom.

Ben-hadad was assisting the Northern Kingdom of Israel at the time, making them too much of a force for Asa to confront on his own. Asa hoped the large amount of wealth he sent would change Syria's allegiance (2 Chronicles 16:2–3).

Absent from the text is any indication of Asa asking the Lord for wisdom or help in resisting King Baasha's actions against Judah. Centuries later, the Lord, through the prophet Jeremiah, warned against such misplaced trust: "Cursed is the man who trusts in man and makes flesh his strength, whose heart turns away from the Lord" (Jeremiah 17:5). Asa's plan revealed a heart that had turned away from relying on the Lord. He forgot the Lord's promise to always be with him, and instead depended on his own ingenuity when facing the new threat.

Asa's plan worked. When the Syrian king attacked Israel, King Baasha abandoned his fortification of Ramah. Not only did this reopen the key trade route, but it also enabled Asa to use the building materials left behind by the king of Israel to reinforce his cities in Judah (2 Chronicles 16:4–6). Asa may have thought that all had turned out well—that is, until the Lord confronted him regarding his dependence on Syria rather than on Himself.

Asa's Harsh Response

Despite the success of Asa's strategy, the Lord saw the king's behavior for what it was: confidence in human strength rather than on His. So the Lord sent a prophet named Hanani to confront Asa regarding both his forgetfulness and his unfaithfulness. The seer reminded the king of his past reliance on the Lord, and how, with the Lord's help, Judah had defeated the great army of the Ethiopians. Because he had trusted God, God had given Asa a great victory over the invading army (2 Chronicles 16:7–8).

Hanani concluded his message to the king with these words:

> For the eyes of the LORD run to and fro throughout the whole
> earth, to give strong support to those whose heart is blameless
> toward him. You have done foolishly in this, for from now on
> you will have wars. (2 Chronicles 16:9)

God was watching as Asa put his trust in a foreign king rather than
in Him. If the king had turned to the Lord when he faced the challenge
from King Baasha, the Lord surely would have helped him. He was
ready to strongly support the king in his efforts against the threat posed
by the Northern Kingdom.

Asa's unfaithfulness meant he and his nation would be involved in
wars for the remaining years of his reign. He may have thought he had
purchased lasting peace for his kingdom, but that was not the case.

King Asa's response to the prophet's message is bewildering. Instead
of humbling himself before the Lord, the king responded harshly. Not
only did he put Hanani in prison, but he also "inflicted cruelties upon
some of the people at the same time" (2 Chronicles 16:10). Had they
also sided with the prophet and thus incurred the king's wrath?

The king never repented or turned back to the Lord during the
remaining five years of his life. Even when a disease afflicted his feet,
he refused to seek help from the Lord. Instead, he trusted solely in
his own resources—the doctors who attended to him (2 Chronicles
16:11–12).

Regarding Asa's turn from being a man of faith, Charles Spurgeon, the great nineteenth-century preacher and Bible scholar, said the
following:

> The power of Ethiopia was broken before him, and Judah's armies
> returned laden with the spoil. You would not have thought that
> a man who could perform that grand action would become, a
> little after, full of unbelief; but the greatest faith of yesterday will

not give us confidence for today, unless the fresh springs which are in God shall overflow again.[17]

Persevering to the End

Like the racehorse Always Dreaming, Asa's performance faded at the end of his race and he failed to finish strong. He began neglecting the Lord as the source of his strength and wisdom, instead relying on his own ingenuity and resources.

Had the king not turned away from God, he would have been more like another famous racehorse, Secretariat, who won the Triple Crown in 1973. In the final event, the Belmont Stakes, the horse jumped ahead of the rest early on and held a lead that continually grew to a record-setting margin of victory at the finish line. Secretariat's strong finish that day amazed everyone in the horse-racing world. Unlike King Asa, Secretariat grew stronger, not weaker, as the race continued.

What can help us persevere to the end rather than allow our strength and trust in the Lord to fade as did Asa? There are three particular dangers we must watch for and avoid:

1. Familiarity—Getting Too Comfortable about Faith

I grew up in a Bible-believing home and gave my heart to the Lord at the age of seven. I can't remember a time when I didn't know what Jesus did for me or a time when I failed to believe He was anything but who He claimed to be. Such familiarity, however, often works against me; it diminishes my sense of wonder for all my Savoir accomplished on my behalf.

The people in Nazareth rejected Jesus during His earthly ministry because of their familiarity with Him. After listening to Him as He taught in their synagogue one day, the people of his hometown responded negatively, saying, "Is not this the carpenter, the son of Mary and brother of James and Joses and Judas and Simon? And are not his sisters here with us?" (Mark 6:3). In other words, they were asking, "How could the boy we watched grow up be the long-awaited Messiah?" They couldn't believe Jesus was indeed the Christ.

We face a similar danger in our relationship with the Lord. After walking with Him for many years, many of us start taking Him for granted. We've heard about His death on the cross and the Resurrection so many times those accounts may no longer move our hearts as they once did. The Gospel message may no longer capture our imagination or motivate us.

I can't say for certain that Asa had become so familiar with worshipping the Lord that he lost track of its meaning. I do know, however, that it's a real danger for me, and I suspect it is as well for others who have walked with Christ for much of their lives. We fall into a pattern of taking all His blessings for granted, and we often fail to consider what our lives would be without Jesus and His redeeming love. Like the church in Ephesus, we lose our first love for the Lord (Revelation 2:4).

The Lord knows we are forgetful people. What did He say when He instituted the practice of Communion? "Do this...in remembrance of me" (1 Corinthians 11:25). Although celebrating the Lord's Supper can become something we do out of habit, it's meant to focus our hearts—again and again—on what Jesus accomplished on the cross. By partaking in the sacred ritual, we *remember* Jesus' supreme sacrifice on our behalf. He took the punishment we deserve upon Himself.

While there is no easy antidote for the problems that can come from being overly familiar, or too comfortable, in our faith lives, there are a few things we can do that will help us in this regard.

First, thanking the Lord for everything—for all of His blessings—reminds us of His importance. Prayer involves so much more than presenting Him with our requests. Voicing praise, adoration, and thanksgiving reminds us anew of the ways we benefit from His presence. Such worship renews our appreciation for all He has done.

Second, worshipful music helps us refocus our hearts on the Lord.

Whether we're singing with others during a worship service or when we are alone, songs can remind us of the countless ways God has blessed us.

I enjoy a combination of modern worship tunes along with the hymns of my past, which remind me of God's grace and my salvation. The older songs often have lyrics that bring to mind great biblical doctrines.

2. Forgetting—God's Past Faithfulness

When the king of Israel sought to cut off a key trade route for Judah, Asa turned to Syria for help rather than rely upon the Lord. Had he forgotten about the Lord's miraculous deliverance when an army of one million had come against him? Didn't he remember what God did on that occasion, causing that great imposing force to flee? Yet when faced with a new and much less severe challenge, Asa didn't factor God's previous deliverance into his response. He seemingly forgot all the Lord had done for him in the past.

What about you? If you have walked with the Lord for years, you probably remember several times when the Lord delivered you from peril or sickness, or rescued you in the midst of difficult circumstances. What about the time He provided for your needs just when you needed it the most?

In preparation for writing this chapter, I listened to a sermon by Christian evangelist David Wilkerson titled "Remembering Your Deliverance."[18] As Wilkerson preached on the importance of remembering God's past deliverances in our lives, he told the story of David and Goliath. As David prepared to go against the giant, he told Saul about the times he had killed a lion and bear with the Lord's help (1 Samuel 17:34–37). Remembering what God had done through him previously and voicing those past victories helped give David the courage it took to stand up to the formidable giant.

The point of Wilkerson's sermon was to encourage those in his church to remember what the Lord had done for them. I decided to

take his advice and reflect on memories of times when God showed up
for me in unforgettable ways:

- **Answered prayers:** I remember God providing answers to my
  prayers throughout the years. Some of my prayers were as simple
  as asking for His help in remembering something. Others were
  much more significant, such as asking Him for calmness when
  plagued by worries and fear.
- **Peace about my future:** I remember spending many sleepless
  nights wondering how I could pay all the bills. In response to
  my pleas, the Lord gave me an amazing sense of peace and far
  more provisions than I needed as I meditated on Scripture and
  relevant promises.
- **Health and strength:** I remember when I needed health and
  strength at a critical time in my life, and the Lord delivered both
  in abundance.
- **Protection from harm:** I remember slamming on the brakes
  one day after an SUV pulled onto the road in front of me. As
  my foot hit the pedal, I was one hundred percent convinced I
  would hit the other vehicle and cause serious injuries to both
  of us drivers. Instead of the almost-certain impact coming to
  pass, my car stopped one foot short of the SUV's side door. I sat
  behind the wheel for several moments in stunned silence trying
  to absorb the magnitude of the Lord's deliverance.

An effective antidote to forgetfulness is rehearsing the Lord's answers
to prayers over the years. It gives us hope for the times ahead and reminds
us of our constant need to depend on His strength in all things. As Wilkerson pointed out in his sermon, recalling what God has done gives us
courage to face the "giants" that threaten us from time to time.

For those who are new in your relationship with the Lord, don't forget you have access to countless biblical examples of those who achieved
great victories by trusting the Lord. While the focus of this book has

been on the bad guys of the Bible, Scripture provides a multitude of examples of the "good guys" as well—those whom God delivered in response to their faith in Him.

3. Pride—Taking Credit for God's Triumphs

When we forget God's preeminent role in seeing us through difficult challenges, we face the danger of thinking *we* are responsible for bringing about our past triumphs. Pride thus becomes an ever-present hazard that causes us to relish our own strength rather than being thankful for the Lord's. "If I successfully accomplished something on my own once, I can do it again," or so we think. Such pride moves us away from a close relationship with the Lord.

During the twenty-five years of peace that settled through the land after the Lord delivered Judah from the advancing Ethiopians, Asa forgot what God had done for the king and his people. As year after year passed, Asa increasingly saw himself as being responsible for the calmness his kingdom was experiencing. Then, when he faced the crisis that came toward the end of his reign, he did not turn to the Lord. He mistakenly believed he could manage the challenge himself.

When the prophet confronted Asa, rather than humbly admit his sin, the king responded angrily and had him imprisoned. Proverbs 16:18 says, "Pride goes before destruction, and a haughty spirit before a fall." Like King Asa, when we become too confident of our ability to stand on our own, we can be sure that danger lurks on the horizon. When we presumptuously rely on our own strength, we set ourselves up for a fall.

During my college days, I took a young woman bowling one evening. While Karen struggled to get the hang of it at first, I got off to one of my best starts ever, bowling strikes or spares in every frame. Flush with overconfidence, I asked her to watch my form during the next frame.

I still remember my embarrassment when my "form" sent the ball rolling right into the gutter. The words of Proverbs 16:18 immediately came to mind as I turned and humbly walked back toward Karen, who had seen my every move. And, wouldn't you know it—she beat me in the second game! While pride may not always lead to such a rapid— or closely watched—downfall, it never fails to catch up with us in the future.

Walking with God

What does Asa teach us about our walk with God? He shows us the danger of forgetting all the Lord has done, which causes us to rely on our own strength to meet new challenges.

Walking with the Lord involves more than resting on the faith of our past; it requires that we continue to rely on the sole source of our strength, the Holy Spirit. The Spirit reminds us of God's past work in our lives and renews our strength as we pursue closer fellowship with and trust in the Lord. As we recall the ways He has seen us through previous challenges, He refreshes our confidence in Him and sharpens our awareness of the constant need to depend on Him in the future.

The Christian life is a marathon; it's not a sprint. If you find yourself running well early in the race, keep looking to the Lord, and never forget that you're fueled by His power alone.

Walking with the Lord means we should never stop relying on Him for the strength to get through every day; we mustn't ever forget our moment-by-moment need to depend on Him.

STUDY GUIDE

Chapter 11

Asa: The King Who Started Fast, Finished Last

Passages: 1 Kings 15:9–24; 2 Chronicles 14–16
Key verses: Revelation 12:4; Proverbs 16:18

Questions for discussion:

1. How did Asa begin his reign in Judah in a manner reminiscent of King David?
2. What did Asa's prayer in response to the Ethiopian invasion reveal about the king's faith at the time?
3. How did Asa respond differently to the threat posed by King Baasha much later in his reign?
4. What do we learn from Asa's response to Hanani about how far the king had drifted from his faith in the Lord?
5. How can years or even decades of being familiar with the Gospel cause us to drift away from our faith in the Lord?
6. What do we learn from the account of David and Goliath about recounting God's past victories in our lives?
7. What ways has God carried you through difficult circumstances or answered your prayers? Consider keeping a list of those times as a way of remembering God's past faithfulness to you?

Study Guide

Chapter 7

8. How does pride cause us to rely on ourselves when we should be resting on the Lord's strength and deliverance?

Key lesson: Asa's life illustrates the danger of forgetting all that the Lord has done for us, which causes us to rely on our own strength to meet the challenges we face. Walking with the Lord means we never stop relying on Him for the strength we need to get us through every day; we never forget our moment-by-moment need to totally rely upon Him.

12

CAIN

THE BROTHER WHO REJECTED GOD'S FORGIVENESS

*Thus says the LORD: "Let not the wise man boast in his wisdom,
let not the mighty man boast in his might, let not the rich man
boast in his riches, but let him who boasts boast in this, that he
understands and knows me, that I am the LORD who practices
steadfast love, justice, and righteousness in the earth. For in these
things I delight, declares the LORD."*

—JEREMIAH 9:23–24

It was early in the morning when he finally arrived home and sat down
next to his worried wife. He had stayed at the office all night poring
through the evidence he had amassed during his two-year investigation.
He had hoped to arrive at a different conclusion, but all the facts in the
case pointed in the opposite direction.

Looking at his deeply troubled spouse, he simply said, "I believe."
He then told her of his quest to disprove the Resurrection of Jesus and
thereby debunk Christianity once and for all. As I watched this scene in
the movie *The Case for Christ*, tears came to my eyes as the man prayed

for the first time in his life, confessing his sins and asking Jesus to be his Savior.

The movie dramatizes journalist Lee Strobel's passionate and often angry efforts to prove that Christianity rests on a hoax. As an investigative reporter for the *Chicago Tribune*, he employed all his skills and tapped into all the resources available to equip him in his quest. After two years of gathering information and examining all the data, Lee realized he could not dispute the fact of Jesus' Resurrection. Instead, the evidence proved Jesus did indeed arise from the grave, just as Scripture says. Thus, He is *everything* He claims to be.

Since that day, Lee Strobel has become a world-famous author and spokesperson proclaiming the reality of the Resurrection and saving faith. He vigorously defends the claims of the Christian faith, the very truths he once fought stubbornly to cancel, but could not do so.

Strobel's journey stands in stark contrast to the path taken by the next character in our study. Whereas Strobel began his investigation as an avowed atheist, Cain began life knowing God existed. He had verbal conversations with Him and even argued with Him at times. He could never deny God's existence. Yet, in spite of all this, he rejected God's offer of forgiveness and, along with it, eternal life. He spurned God's way of salvation, choosing to approach Him in his own way.

Cain brings us face to face with the most important decision we can make. How do we respond to God and His gracious provision for our salvation? Even if we somehow avoid making the mistakes of the other "bad guys" in this book, it won't matter whatsoever at the end of our lives if we make the same error as Cain did by rejecting the only path to eternal life that the Lord offers.

God Rejects Cain's Sacrifice

Cain, Adam and Eve's firstborn son, is the third person mentioned in Scripture. His birth brought an exclamation of excitement from Eve:

"With the help of the LORD I have brought forth a man" (Genesis 4:1, NIV). She optimistically saw her son as the one God promised would defeat the serpent (see Genesis 3:15).

By the time Cain's brother, Abel, was born, Eve didn't appear to be as hopeful. The name "Abel" means "a fleeting breath" or "meaninglessness." The book of Ecclesiastes uses that very word to express the vanity and fleeting nature of life. Was the name prophetic of the shortness of Abel's life or just a sign of Eve's growing despair after being exiled from Paradise? As time had progressed, she apparently realized Cain was *not* the answer she had hoped for, and her anguish carried over to Abel as well.

The two brothers pursued different occupations. Abel tended to cattle while Cain worked the soil (Genesis 4:2). Nothing in the text suggests Abel's work was more acceptable to God than Cain's; both were honorable jobs.

The biblical text doesn't say what prompted the offerings the brothers took to the Lord or what led to the specific gifts each presented to Him on this occasion. Scripture simply says Abel took the "firstborn of his flock" to the Lord, while Cain offered God something he had grown, simply referred to as "the fruit of the ground." God accepted Abel and his sacrifice, but rejected Cain and his offering (Genesis 4:3–5).

Why did God reject Cain's sacrifice? Many believe God had asked for a blood sacrifice. They suggest Cain refused to go along with this request and offered a sample of his own produce rather than go to Abel and purchase the required sacrificial animal.

Others see a difference in the quality of what each man took to the Lord. Cain merely offered a portion of his yield, while Abel chose the "firstborn," representing the best of his livestock (Genesis 4:3–4). Cain's rebellious spirit thus revealed itself in his unwillingness to offer his best to the Lord, while Abel's obedient spirit was reflected by his offering of the choicest of all his animals. This theory is possible, as it reflects the attitude of each toward God.

Although the text doesn't state the exact reason for the rejection, it suggests the difference wasn't only with each sacrifice, but with the one offering it as well. "The LORD looked with favor on Abel and his offering, but on Cain and his offering he did not look with favor" (Genesis 4:4–5). Notice how Moses, the writer of Genesis, draws our attention to the giver as well as the gift; God rejected Cain *and* his offering. His problem went much deeper than taking the wrong gifts to the Lord; it stemmed from his heart.

Regarding the brothers' offerings, the writer of Hebrews said: "By faith Abel offered God a better sacrifice than Cain did" (Hebrews 11:4, NIV). Throughout Hebrews 11, we see that the "heroes of faith" demonstrated their trust through obedience to God's Word, to what the Lord specifically told them to do. Cain displayed his lack of faith by refusing to approach the Lord in the prescribed way. Cain wanted to do it his way, which somehow revealed his disobedient heart.

Cain responded angrily to the Lord's rejection of his offering. Showing both love and mercy, God gave him another chance, but warned him of the consequences if he continued to rebel. The Lord depicted sin as a "devouring beast" waiting to pounce on Cain (Genesis 4:6–7).

This has a double meaning: If Cain obeyed, the sin offering (an animal) was right there waiting for him to present as his sacrifice. If not, his rejection of God's provision for his sin would further harden his unrepentant heart.

Cain refused God's offer of salvation. His outward rebellion displayed the true intent of his heart. He did not trust the Lord, and as a result, he never came to know Him as his Savior.

Cain Kills His Brother

Sometime after God's rejection of his offering, Cain lured Abel to a field and killed him (Genesis 4:8). It's difficult to imagine that murder could take place in just the second generation of humans after Creation, but it did, and it continues to be the deadly impact sin has on the human race.

The killing revealed more than just Cain's envy of Abel; it signified a blow against God and His mercy. Rather than accept the second chance the Lord so graciously gave him, Cain devised a plot to get even with Abel—and teach God a lesson at the same time.

Still offering Cain a chance to seek His mercy, the Lord asked a simple question: "Where is Abel your brother?" Even after Cain's gruesome act, the Lord approached him with great compassion. God didn't need the information, as He had of course seen what happened. However, Cain needed a chance to confess his crime and ask for forgiveness.

Instead of owning up to what he had done, Cain responded to the Lord with an arrogant lie ("I don't know") and his famous sarcastic question: "Am I my brother's keeper?" (Genesis 4:9). How could Cain be so audacious? Did he really believe he could conceal the murder from God?

The Lord then announced that the blood of Abel was crying out to Him "from the ground" (Genesis 4:10). Next, in response to Cain's lack of repentance, God issued His judgment: The land Cain had polluted with his brother's blood would no longer yield crops. He would be a wanderer and fugitive for the rest of his life (Genesis 4:11–12).

Cain, however, remained defiant and unrepentant; he protested that the punishment would be too much for him to bear (Genesis 4:13). Rather than fearing God, he complained about how others might respond to his crime ("they'll kill me"; Genesis 4:14). He failed to grasp the seriousness of his sin and amazingly remained unremorseful about killing Abel.

By this time, Cain surely had other brothers and sisters who might have sought to avenge Abel's death (Genesis 4:15–16). As a result, God gave Cain another gracious response: A sign to protect him.

Here again we see the Lord's willingness to deal mercifully with even the most unrepentant of sinners. Even after Cain's horrible crime, God kept open the door to forgiveness...but Cain never entered it.

Getting to Know God

Cain's behavior illustrates the danger of attempting to approach God on our own terms. Many people know about God and believe many things about Jesus and His teachings, but, like Cain, they continue to reject the offer of forgiveness for their sins. They tragically trust themselves or their "good" behavior more than they trust Jesus.

Believers can make the same mistake. The pride and self-sufficiency Cain demonstrated is a difficult habit to break. Any time we depend on our own goodness or religious behavior to merit favor with God, we follow Cain's example.

What can we learn from Cain that will help us *know God* personally rather than just *know about* Him? What will help followers of Christ remember the truths of the Gospel when we begin to look away from the Savior and attempt to make life work on our own?

1. Remember Jesus Is the Only Path to Eternal Life.

On this side of the cross, we have a huge advantage over Cain. Though we don't necessarily have audible conversations with God as Cain did, we have Scripture that contains the record of Jesus' death on the cross for our sins as well as His glorious Resurrection. We also have the New Testament accounts describing Jesus, through His apostles, revealing all the wonders of His saving message of grace. The books of Romans and Ephesians give the wondrous details of the Gospel—we receive eternal life as a free gift simply by grace through faith in our Savior, the Lord Jesus.

In the account of Cain and Abel, we don't have the details of God's instructions regarding their sacrifices. Some disagreement exists as to why God chose Abel's offering over Cain's. One theme, however, remains the same no matter what: *Cain decided to approach God in his own way.* He steadfastly refused to listen to Him and constantly sought to do things his way.

God rejected Cain because of his unbelief, not because of his sins.

Cain never trusted the Lord. He refused to admit his sinfulness and hence rejected the sacrifice the Lord offered to provide him with in order to pay for his sins.

Cain represents all who follow the pattern of proclaiming their own goodness and rejecting Jesus' sacrifice for their many transgressions.

On the night before His Crucifixion, Jesus clarified for all time that He is the *only* way of salvation: "I am the way, and the truth, and the life. No one comes to the Father except through me" (John 14:6). There is no other way to approach the Father except through Jesus and the blood He shed for us on the cross.

A few months after Jesus spoke those words, the Apostle Peter confirmed: "There is salvation in no one else, for there is no other name under heaven given among men by which we must be saved" (Acts 4:12). True Christianity is *radically exclusive*; no one can find eternal life apart from Christ.

If there was any other way for God to save us, do you really think that Jesus, God in the flesh, would have had to endure such a horrific and painful death on the cross? If being obedient to the Father could have even remotely resulted in our acceptance by Him, would He really have required His Only Son to suffer such intense agony with the horrific flogging, mocking, and the tremendous emotional pain of His momentary separation from the Father?

If the world's religions could have somehow provided any saving merit whatsoever, why would it have been necessary for Jesus to suffer? Furthermore, if Jesus could have saved us simply with His teachings and by His example, He certainly wouldn't have gone to the cross.

However, because there was no other way to receive eternal life, God the Father allowed His Son to endure a horrifying and brutal death on the cross. And on the third day after that, He arose from death, verifying that He was who He claimed to be and that His Word is eternal (Matthew 24:35). The historical fact of the empty tomb points to only one conclusion: Jesus walked out of the tomb demonstrating the truth of all His claims.

He is the only way to eternal life; He paid the debt for our sins on the cross.

Many scoff at such a teaching. They insist that as long as people have faith, are good, have sincere hearts, they have all it takes to get them to Heaven—even if they don't trust Christ for eternal life.

Those who think in such a way make the same mistake as Cain. They believe they can reject God's Word and approach Him on their own terms. The result is death—both in this earthly life and in eternity.

The Lord's invitation to accept forgiveness of sins and eternal life remains open to all, but those who reject Him and His sacrifice for their sins face never-ending suffering after they die.

I believe the Lord received Abel's sacrifice because it pointed toward Jesus' death as the ultimate sacrifice on the cross. Even if Cain had brought the best of his produce, it still would have represented human effort, not the Lord's way. Cain, like multitudes of people after him, tried to gain acceptance from the Lord on his own terms, ignoring God's clear instructions.

2. God Saves Us by Grace Alone Through faith.

A few years back, an investment banking firm used this slogan in its commercials: "They make money the old-fashioned way. They earn it." While that saying may apply to financial investments, it certainly doesn't pertain to salvation. Tragically, many people follow Cain's example, insisting on trying to secure eternal life in Heaven by doing things the "old-fashioned way"—earning it. Rather than trusting the Lord by accepting His gift of forgiveness, they persist in their efforts to gain eternal life their way, but they end up on the road to death.

In Ephesians 2:8–9 Paul said: "It is by grace you have been saved, through faith—and this not from yourselves, it is the gift of God—not by works, so that no one can boast" (NIV). We can't obtain eternal life through our own efforts; it's impossible. Salvation is a gift; it comes solely through faith on the basis of God's grace, mercy, and love for us. Whenever we add something to that formula, it ceases to become a gift.

At one of his crusades, nineteenth-century evangelist Dwight L. Moody made a free offer of a brand-new Bible (worth about twenty dollars at the time) as an illustration that salvation is completely based on God's grace and not on what we do. He believed someone in the audience would accept his offer, but the one who approached him wasn't comfortable with receiving the Bible for free. Moody suggested that person might feel better by giving him a penny for the Bible. What if he gave it to him for a penny? As soon as he got home, he could brag about purchasing the Bible for just one cent.

The evangelist compared that illustration to someone contributing the least amount of effort to salvation; it would soon become an opportunity for boasting. Moody correctly summed up the human tendency to overestimate our contributions. When it comes to our salvation, we contribute *absolutely nothing*. Even the faith we exercise comes as a gift from the Lord.

Cain wanted God to accept the fruit of his own labor. He hoped others would see that he had merited favor with the Lord by offering his produce. He hoped the Lord's acceptance of his offering would give him a reason to boast about what he had gotten for himself, just like the person in Moody's illustration.

Saving faith signifies that we recognize the absolute helplessness of our condition as well as realize it is Christ—and Him alone—who can save us. God says if we put our trust in Jesus, He will forgive our sins and give us eternal life (John 3:16; Acts 10:43). We cannot and must not depend on ourselves. We can only find salvation by forming a relationship with the Savior. Religious behavior and good works will leave us on the outside looking in and far, far away from the saving grace we so desperately need.

We need a Savior; we need the One who bore our sin and gives us His righteousness in its place, just as Paul wrote in 2 Corinthians 5:21:

For our sake he made him to be sin who knew no sin, so that in
him we might become the righteousness of God.

This is the great exchange: Jesus paid for all our sins, and in return
He assigned His righteousness to us. When we realize the enormity of
our sin and the priceless nature of what it means to stand in His sin-
less perfection, we realize we have no reason to boast—either now or in
eternity.

3. We Remain in His Favor Forever

One of the toughest lessons to learn is that once we come to know Christ
as Savior, we remain in His favor forever; absolutely nothing we do can
change our standing of eternal acceptance. One of Satan's most successful lies is that we must strive continually to earn God's love, even after we
become born-again followers of Jesus. Thus, we never feel free because
we always rely on our own efforts, even in the midst of trials, to obtain
God's blessings.

In their book *Hudson Taylor's Spiritual Secret*, Howard and Geraldine
Taylor wrote about how Hudson Taylor learned to depend on the Lord
during many afflictions. Taylor labored for several years as a missionary
to China, believing he was trusting solely in Christ to meet his needs.
He did not, however, experience real joy or freedom in his ministry until
a letter arrived from a friend with these words: "It is not by trusting my
own faithfulness, but by looking away to the Faithful One!"[19]

Those words altered Hudson's life; they enabled him to draw upon
the power of the Lord rather than lean on his own strength. Taylor discovered that the source of his hope was in Christ's unfailing love for him.
He learned to rest on God's steadfast love rather than his own faithfulness, and as a result he experienced a renewal of joyfulness and energy
for serving the Lord.

In his book *Knowing God*, J. I. Packer spoke of God's unfailing love
and how it motivates us to serve Him:

This is momentous knowledge. There is unspeakable comfort—
the sort of comfort that energises, be it said, not enervates—in
knowing that God is constantly taking knowledge of me in love,
and watching over me for my good.[20]

Even though we know God saves us by His mercy and grace alone,
it's easy to fall into the trap of thinking we need to keep being good to
remain in His favor. As Packer stated, there is "unspeakable comfort" in
realizing that, despite everything He knows about us, God responds to
us with unfailing love. He sees us as totally righteous and never stops
seeking our well-being in all things.

When I was in college, I remember having a conversation in which
a friend recounted something good that had happened to him. Another
student responded with these words: "You must have had your devotions today."

At the time, I didn't realize how much this statement contradicts
the biblical truths of the Gospel. While it's great to spend time with the
Lord each day, "doing our devotions" is never the reason God acts on
our behalf or blesses us. All of His favor upon us flows exclusively from
His unfailing love—never from our behavior, regardless of how "good"
it might have been earlier in the day.

Believers remain forever in God's favor *solely because of Jesus*. Romans
8:1 says: "There is therefore now no condemnation for those who are
in Christ Jesus." We will always be secure in Him, and therefore we'll
always have His approval.

Those who say we can lose our salvation or "fall away" from our faith
make the same terrible mistake as Cain. They add works to salvation
equation and thereby deny the Apostle Paul's words in Ephesians 2:8–9.
They put the emphasis on themselves rather than where it belongs, on
our loving Savior.

Our permanent, righteous standing before God is all because of
grace from start to finish. Don't let anyone cancel your security as a
redeemed child of God.

God always sees us as His dear, righteous children; never for a second will He ever consider us as anything else. This *never* changes, because it always depends on His faithfulness, not ours. We remain secure only because of His love for us.

Walking with God

What does Cain teach us about our walk with God? He shows us the necessity of truly knowing God and of having a saving relationship with Him.

Where are you in your spiritual journey? Have you taken the step of putting your faith in Christ? Or, are you like Cain, depending on your own goodness to try to merit eternal life?

Romans 10:13 says: "Everyone who calls on the name of the Lord will be saved." Jesus is most assuredly the *only* way of salvation, the *only* path to forgiveness of sins and eternal life in Paradise. As we turn to Him in faith, asking Him to forgive our sins, He saves us because of His grace and great love. It never ever depends on us.

Even as born-again followers of Jesus, we must avoid following Cain's example. We are forever secure in God's unmerited favor, not in our continuing efforts to please Him.

Our walk with God relies on the fact that His love will never fail us. We know that, even in the worst of circumstances, it will sustain us. Once in Christ, nothing, and I mean nothing, can separate us from His love and redeeming grace. If you haven't read Romans 8:31–39 recently, please do so now, basking in the comfort of knowing that, in Christ, we are "more than conquerors" regardless of what comes our way.

His grace is so much greater than our failures; we never fall beyond the restoring touch of the Savior. Walking with such confidence is what it means for believers to avoid the trap of following in the way of Cain.

STUDY GUIDE

Chapter 12

Cain: The Brother Who Rejected God's Forgiveness

Passage: Genesis 4
Key verses: Hebrews 11:4; John 14:6; Ephesians 2:8–10

Questions for discussion:

1. What are some reasons God accepted Abel's sacrifice but rejected Cain's?
2. How was the murder of Abel also a blow against God?
3. How did Cain display a continued defiant and unrepentant attitude toward God?
4. What's the key danger that we see from Cain's example?
5. What does John 14:6 say about the exclusivity of the Christian faith?
6. Why do you think so many people today scoff at the news that Jesus is the only way to eternal life?
7. What does Ephesians 2:8–10 indicate about the role of faith and works in regard to our salvation?
8. How does God's unending love motivate us to serve Him?
9. Have you placed your faith in Jesus—who He is and what He did for us? Is your hope of eternal life based solely on Jesus or only on yourself?

STUDY GUIDE

Chapter 12

10. If you are born again, do you rest in the Lord's unending favor and love?

Key lesson: The example of Cain warns us against attempting to approach God on our own terms. On this side of the cross, God tells us that Jesus is the only path to eternal life.

13

JOHN MARK

THE MISSIONARY WHO BAILED
(BUT RETURNED TO FAITHFUL SERVICE)

*Therefore, my beloved brothers, be steadfast, immovable, always
abounding in the work of the Lord, knowing that in the Lord
your labor is not in vain.*

—1 Corinthians 15:58

I never thought I would see it happen. If you had asked me before 2016
if I thought it were possible, I would have said, "No! Absolutely not!"
While you might think that's a bit pessimistic (okay, extremely so), it
hadn't happened in more than a hundred years, and I didn't see it as a
possibility in my lifetime.

However, in 2016, the Cubs won the World Series for the first time
in 108 years. They hadn't even played in the fall classic since 1945. Yet
there they were, going up against the Cleveland Indians for the prize that
had eluded them for over a century. And amazingly, they won it all in
the dramatic seventh-game comeback.

Having been a fan of the Cubs since the mid-1960s, I believed the team would always fall short when it came to reaching or winning the World Series. That's what made their 2016 season and eventual championship so endearing to many people like me. A team that had failed so many times finally ended up on top of the baseball world.

We all like stories of those who triumph after failure, who don't give up despite the odds. In September 2013, for example, Diana Nyad became the first person to swim the 110 miles from Cuba to Florida without the benefit of a shark cage. The sixty-four-year-old woman had tried to do so and failed on four previous occasions. This time, however, she successfully swam the entire distance.

I have included John Mark in this study because he represents someone who did not let an early failure in ministry deter him from effectively serving the Lord at a later time. Despite deserting Paul on his first missionary journey, he eventually became dear and valuable to the apostle. We don't know the details of what happened during the intervening years, but we do know John Mark didn't let his initial failure keep him from pressing forward. *He did not let it define him.*

I remember as a child hearing a sermon on 1 Corinthians 9:24–27. The pastor repeatedly warned that once a person fails in ministry, they end up "on the shelf." Those may not have been his precise words, but they were what I took away from the message.

Was God just waiting for me to fail? If I messed up once, would that be the end of my effectiveness for the Lord? Would I end up being "on the shelf" somewhere forever?

This message stuck with me because, starting from the age of eleven, I believed the Lord was calling me to full-time service. As a result, the overly legalistic tone of the sermon plagued me for many, many years—long after I knew better.

I feared that one mistake would forever end my value to the Lord. It may even have been one of the reasons my failure as a pastor (which I shared in the introduction) came as such a shock. I mistakenly believed my season of usefulness to the Lord was over. I thought I'd be forever "on the shelf."

This is why I'm so attracted to the story of John Mark—often referred to as simply "Mark." The Lord used him in significant ways despite a glaring shortcoming in the early days of his service.

John Mark's Early Years

John Mark grew up in Jerusalem as the son of Mary—not the mother of Jesus, but another Mary, who was a prominent member of the early Church there. You may remember that her home was the one Peter went directly to after the Lord delivered him from prison. Acts 12:12–17 tells the endearing story of that event: The apostle knocked on the door of Mary's house, where the church had gathered to pray for his safe release from jail. Rhoda, the servant girl who answered the door, recognized Peter's voice, but in her excitement, she didn't let him in. Instead, she rushed to share the good news with those who had been praying for Peter's release. At first, they didn't believe the answer to their prayers was standing right outside their door.

This account tells us Mark grew up in a fairly affluent home for the first century AD. Besides having the resources required to employ a servant, Mary had a room in her residence large enough for several believers to gather to pray and certainly to meet at other times as well. Since Luke identified the home as the "house of Mary" and failed to mention Mark's father, Mary was likely a widow at the time.

In the Gospel he wrote, Mark told a story about a "young man" who was with Jesus at the time of His arrest: "And a young man followed him, with nothing but a linen cloth about his body. And they seized him, but he left the linen cloth and ran away naked" (Mark 14:51–52).

The evidence—based on church tradition and the fact that he included this in his narrative without naming himself, which was a common practice in the first century AD—strongly points to the identity of this young man as being John Mark.

Since he was present with Jesus on the night of His arrest, we can safely assume Mark was a follower of Jesus at the time and had witnessed many events of the Savior's life, especially during His last week in Jerusalem. Mark may have heard Jesus teach at other times as well.

Mark Leaves the Missionary Team

Acts 13:5 indicates John Mark was a team member during the first missionary journey of the Apostle Paul and Barnabas. After the church in Antioch set that pair apart for this work, they picked up Mark along the way to "assist" them in their calling. His inclusion on the team came about because he and Barnabas were cousins (Colossians 4:10).

We're not entirely sure how Mark contributed to the missionary team. In his Gospel, Luke used the same Greek word for "assist" as Mark did; this word refers to being an attendant in a synagogue (Luke 4:20). Because this assistant handled the scrolls of Scripture, some believe Mark carried the scrolls Paul and Barnabas took with them and found the passages they desired to read during the trip. Others believe they included Mark on the journey because of his firsthand knowledge about Christ's life, particularly His last days, arrest, and Resurrection.

It's probable that Mark helped Paul and Barnabas in many ways as they traveled to the island of Cyprus, Barnabas' birthplace. There he witnessed the conversion of the proconsul and the emergence of Paul as the leader of the group. After achieving success in Cyprus, the ministry team sailed to Perga in Pamphylia (Acts 13:6–13).

In Perga, with no explanation given by Luke, John Mark departed and went back to Jerusalem. Why did he leave? We don't know for sure, but commentators offer several possible reasons for his departure:

- Homesickness
- Weariness from the rigors of the trip
- Fear of the dangers ahead
- Unhappiness about leaving Cyprus so soon
- Displeasure with Paul rather than his cousin Barnabas assuming leadership
- Disagreement with the increasing Gentile focus of the trip

Whatever the cause, we know Paul regarded Mark's departure as a shortcoming. When it came time for Paul and Barnabas to return to the churches they had planted on their first journey, Barnabas wanted to again take John Mark. Paul, however, *strongly* opposed including someone who had earlier failed to stay with them (Acts 15:36–41). He clearly regarded Mark's desertion as a failure of character.

Because of the conflict, Paul and Barnabas went in separate directions. Mark sailed to Cyprus with his cousin to continue the work there. Paul added Silas to his team and began retracing the steps of his first missionary journey.

Mark's Return to Faithful Service

Through the brief references to him in the letters Paul later wrote, we see that Mark later returned to great favor in the apostle's eyes. In Colossians 4:10, we read:

Aristarchus my fellow prisoner greets you, and Mark the cousin of Barnabas (concerning whom you have received instructions—if he comes to you, welcome him), and Jesus who is called Justus. These are the only men of the circumcision among my fellow workers for the kingdom of God, and they have been a comfort to me.

This verse tells us a couple of things about Mark and Paul's relationship at this time. First, the two seem to be together at the time of Paul's house arrest in Rome. Second, Paul instructed the Colossians to warmly receive Mark, which indicates the apostle held a highly favorable opinion of him.

In the book of Philemon, which was written at the same time as Colossians, Paul referred to Mark as one of his "fellow workers" (vv. 23–24). Again, we see Paul affirming Mark as a co-laborer.

When Paul wrote Timothy during his second Roman imprisonment, he said: "Get Mark and bring him with you, for he is very useful to me for ministry" (2 Timothy 4:11). So, the same person the apostle refused to include in his second missionary journey was later regarded as "very useful." During the intervening years, Paul's opinion of Mark had changed from "failure" to "useful."

This speaks to the spiritual maturity of both men. Paul was able to put aside his earlier assessment and recognize Mark as a valuable co-laborer on behalf of the Gospel. John Mark didn't let his earlier lapse (in deserting the ministry trip) define him or keep him from further service to the Lord. He went with his cousin on another missionary journey, and later Paul praised Mark for his service to the Lord.

The Apostle Peter later expressed a close connection to John Mark, referring to him as "my son" (1 Peter 5:13). Church history tells us that, in his Gospel account, Mark recorded the recollections of Peter regarding the life of Christ. He may have also contributed what he saw for himself of Jesus' ministry in Jerusalem, particularly in the days leading up to His arrest.

Recovering From Failure

Do you see why I love the story of John Mark? After his early failure, who would have thought he would later become effective in spreading the message about Christ and would write a book the Lord uses to speak to many today?

Our mistakes and shortcomings absolutely do not put us "on the shelf" forever, in terms of the ways the Lord can use us in the future. In His grace, He often restores and uses even broken vessels to proclaim His glory. *Failure does not have to mark the end of our effectiveness for the cause of Christ. Not at all!*

In the Old Testament, we see numerous examples of the Lord using people after they failed Him. I love reading the story of Jacob, because, in spite of his many rough edges, to say the least, the Lord brought him to maturity in the faith—albeit slowly. Moses killed an Egyptian, but forty years later, he led the children of Israel out of Egypt. And who would have thought the Lord could use David so mightily after his sin with Bathsheba?

John Mark is a New Testament example that assures us failure doesn't have to become our identity or end our fruitfulness for the Lord.

What can help us recover from failure and resume a life of faithful service?

1. Remember God Gives Many Second Chances

Mark provides yet another reminder that God often gives us second chances…and often many, many more. We still benefit today from Mark's continued service. Besides writing the Gospel of Mark, tradition credits him with establishing a church in Alexandria, Egypt. Mark not only continued in ministry, but he became valuable in promoting the cause of Christ both then and now.

My own life has followed a similar pattern to that of Mark. As I mentioned in the introduction, circumstances turned my life upside-down as a young pastor. I felt like a total failure when I resigned from the church and pursued a career in corporate finance. I never stopped to consider that the Lord might use me again in any meaningful way.

Since I retired to pursue a full-time writing ministry, the Lord has surprised me and proved my initial assumption to be wrong. I now have a blog, and my book on future things, *The Triumph of the Redeemed*, has been in print for over a year. Its publication was one of my key objectives in retiring.

The Lord has given me a wonderful "second chance" beyond what I could ever have imagined. And He has done it in such a way that I know it's because of Him and definitely not because of me. As I look back, I am extremely thankful for all the tribulations I experienced. During my time as a pastor and in the years afterward, I exuded pride and lacked the spiritual maturity to deal with the fierce storms that came my way. At the time, I thought the multiplied afflictions were far too much for me to endure (and they were). The Lord, however, knew otherwise; He provided just what I needed in order to learn to depend on Him and trust His love and faithfulness.

If you can identify with Mark or me because you also think you've fallen short of God's expectations, take heart. The Lord can still use you! Past failures often become paths to spiritual maturity and even *greater* opportunities for ministry. Fortunately, the Lord doesn't require perfection but hearts eager to serve Him however He leads. He has worked—in spite of my shortcomings and failures—to open a much greater avenue for ministry than I ever thought possible; through my website I reach people all over the world with the blessed hope we have because of His love and truth.

It's important to recognize that failure is not always because of sin; we can experience failures through no fault of our own. However, even if our shortcomings have contributed to what happens to us, the Lord is willing to forgive us in His great mercy and grace, and He can use us to further enlarge His kingdom.

Never forget that God remains faithful to His children, even after they fail.

2. Trust the Lord Alone

What gives us the courage to persevere despite disappointing experiences we've had? I believe it's the assurance that the Lord will work through our efforts and reward our service. When we start depending on ourselves, we find the road before us seems daunting and, at times, impassable. The results of faithful service rest in the hands of the Lord; He alone is our confidence.

In my early days of being a pastor, Proverbs 21:31 became a favorite verse: "The horse is made ready for the day of battle, but the victory belongs to the LORD." While preparation is necessary for teaching God's Word, it's not our efforts that accomplish His purpose. Like preparing a horse for battle, we do our part. After that, it's the Lord who provides any victories that come our way.

Regardless of what God is calling you to do, whether it's teaching in front of many people or welcoming visitors to your church, it helps to remember that our confidence in ministry depends upon the Lord. In 2 Corinthians 3:4–6 Paul says:

> Such is the confidence that we have through Christ toward God. Not that we are sufficient in ourselves to claim anything as coming from us, but our sufficiency is from God, who has made us sufficient to be ministers of a new covenant, not of the letter but of the Spirit. For the letter kills, but the Spirit gives life.

A song that's helped me in this regard is "Voice of Truth" by Casting Crowns. Listening to its lyrics helps me focus on Jesus and reminds me of what God says about me versus the lies and accusations of the devil. While Satan continually reminds me of the many times that I've blown it, Jesus asks me to trust Him once more as He continues to lead me.

3. Serve with an Eternal Perspective

After reminding the Corinthian believers of the certainty of obtaining a resurrected and immortal body when Jesus comes for His Church, the Apostle Paul added another promise: "Therefore, my beloved brothers, be steadfast, immovable, always abounding in the work of the Lord, knowing that in the Lord your labor is not in vain" (1 Corinthians 15:58). We can relax, knowing the Lord will reward us for our labors on His behalf.

We may not see the results of our efforts to serve the Lord; we might even assume at times that nothing happens. Maybe we simply greet people as they walk into church, put a check in the offering plate or give online, or prepare a meal for someone in need. Whether we see any good that comes out of our service or not, we can be sure the Lord sees and will reward us for it.

I love how the Apostle Paul wraps up his discussion of Jesus' appearing in 1 Corinthians 15:50–58 with the assurance that the Lord recognizes all of our service for Him.

> Therefore, my beloved brothers, be steadfast, immovable, always abounding in the work of the Lord, knowing that in the Lord your labor is not in vain.

Even if no one knows what we do for the Lord, we continue seeking to please Him knowing that someday, perhaps soon, He will come for us. The verse above assures that He sees our work on His behalf and will reward it on that day.

Walking with God

What does John Mark teach us about our walk with God? His story inspires us to never let our past shortcomings deter us from seizing current service opportunities the Lord brings our way, whether large or small in scope. We must not let earlier failures define who we are today.

Furthermore, our inadequacies do not have to signal the end of our effectiveness for the Lord. If Mark had let Paul's early opinion of him define him, in all likelihood he would have refused Barnabas' invitation to go with him back to Cyprus. He might have said to himself, "What's the point?" and vanished from the pages of Scripture and church history.

Instead, Mark didn't give up. He went with his cousin on another missionary journey and later became someone Paul praised for his service for the Lord.

Mark's story encourages us because it shows how God can use someone to accomplish great things in spite of past failures. When we read of Mark's departure from the team on the first missionary journey and Paul's great displeasure with him, it's difficult to imagine he would later, with Peter's help, author one of the four Gospel accounts of Jesus' life, become a highly valued co-laborer with Paul, and start a thriving church in North Africa.

In 1941, Winston Churchill gave the commencement speech for the graduating class at Harrow School. While popularly labeled as a short "never give up" talk, his actual words were as follows: "Never give in. Never give in. Never, never, never, never—in nothing great or small, large or petty—never give in, except to convictions of honor and good sense."[21]

John Mark heeded such advice, didn't he? He never gave up in his efforts to serve the Lord, and he inspires us to do the same.

Many of the other men in our study allowed their lapses to define them. Apart from Gehazi, we don't read of them later returning to the Lord in any meaningful way. Thankfully, our failures don't have to be the final chapter in our book. They need not limit our future in serving the Lord.

I am so thankful to the Lord for the *many* second chances He gave me throughout my life, for His calling me yet again to serve Him through my writing—in particular, this book.

STUDY GUIDE

Chapter 13

John Mark: The Missionary Who Bailed
(But Returned to Faithful Service)

Passages: Acts 13:4–13; 15:36–41; Colossians 4:10; 2 Timothy 4:11
Key verses: 1 Corinthians 15:58; 2 Corinthians 3:4–6

Questions for discussion:

1. How might a legalistic attitude sideline us after a failure in serving the Lord?
2. What do we know about the early years of John Mark?
3. Why might Saul and Barnabas have added John Mark to their team, and what seems to have been his role?
4. What stands out to you as possible reasons for John Mark's departure from the team?
5. How does Paul's later praise for John Mark reveal positive aspects of his character as well as that of John Mark?
6. Have you ever benefitted from God giving you a second chance? Are you willing to share what happened?
7. Why is it so important that we place our confidence solely in the Lord as we serve Him?
8. Why is so important that we not let failure define us?

STUDY GUIDE

Chapter 13

9. How does an eternal perspective affect your service for God? Are you ready for Jesus' imminent appearing to take you home?
10. In what way(s) does the story of John Mark encourage you?

Key lesson: John Mark inspires us to never let past failures deter us from seizing the current service opportunities the Lord brings our way.

LIFE WILL NEVER GO AS PLANNED

I am aware that, for some people, life closely follows what they expect it to be. If you're like me, however, that's definitely not the case. Life rarely goes as planned for many of us; it's far too uncertain for that. My life hasn't resembled my initial ideas for it in any way, shape, or form; it's not even close to what I thought it might be. However, despite everything, the Lord has blessed me beyond what I ever could have imagined.

I continually thank Him for His over-the-top goodness to me and for the fact that my life didn't go the way I planned. I'm glad He took me on a great detour from my intentions for the future.

This book is my declaration of God's over-the-top goodness and faithfulness to me. *He alone is the reason I did not go down some of the disastrous roads many of the guys in this book traveled when my life took a disastrous turn.*

Several of the men we looked at give us hope. In many instances, God graciously gave them opportunities—second chances—to turn

195

back to Him. But all of them, except for John Mark, continued on the path that earned them a place as one of the "bad guys of the Bible."

As a result of living with temporal and self-glorifying agendas, they lost the opportunity to lead lives of eternal significance, even though in some cases, such as Esau's, they obtained outward success in terms of great wealth and power.

During our lives, we will face many of the obstacles encountered by those in our study. We will feel the negative emotions that gripped their souls and led to their unwise decisions. People will get in the way of the happiness we long for and believe we deserve, and we will feel the urge to lash out against them rather than trust the Lord's plans for us.

Others will mistreat us and even lie about us. *How dare they define me in such a way?*

In Genesis 50:20, Joseph spoke the following remarkable words to his brothers, who at the time feared he might exact revenge on them after their father Jacob's death:

> As for you, you meant evil against me, but God meant it for
> good, to bring it about that many people should be kept alive,
> as they are today.

The word for "meant" in both instances above comes from the Hebrew word *chashab*, which assumes a planning process—a calculation with a purpose. Out of jealousy, Joseph's brothers sold him to "Midianite traders," also referred to as "Ishmaelites," who passed by after they had thrown him into a pit (Genesis 37:25–28). When the merchants reached Egypt, they sold him to Potiphar, an Egyptian official (Genesis 39:1). Thirteen years later, Joseph interpreted a dream for Pharaoh, who then elevated him to second in command in Egypt (Genesis 41).

There was evil intent behind the selling of Joseph into slavery, but God sovereignly used the actions of Joseph's brothers to later save many people from death during the great famine of that time. In the end, their own evil conniving saved them from starvation.

Even when others harm us with malicious objectives, as with Joseph's brothers, it never thwarts the Lord's purposes for us. The other sons of Jacob thought they were acting of their own free will to sell Joseph into slavery, and in a sense they were. But all along, God intended for Joseph's position as a slave to serve a greater purpose: keeping many people alive, including the children of Israel, who grew into a mighty nation while in Egypt.

Cancel This

Many use the phrase "cancel culture" to describe the widespread effort to eliminate a biblical worldview from all areas of life today. Unfortunately, many churches have succumbed to the world's effort to replace the standards of God's Word with an "anything goes" mentality. People who live this way trade bondage to the laws of God for slavery to the "woke" crowd they seek to please.

The Church needs men and women who resist society's effort to subvert all of the Lord's moral standards. As New Testament saints, we do this by daily putting the truths of the Gospel into practice. No one can "cancel" the impact of a life driven by these truths, nor can they eliminate the glorious hope that motivates us to stay close to our Savior.

Most of the men in this study shipwrecked their lives by letting unrestrained desires and emotions rule their responses to God and others. They overlooked the impossibility of cancelling His truths as well as the outcome of seeking to do so. Tragically, they allowed an earthbound focus to obscure God's plan for their lives both now and in eternity.

Danger in Letting Negative Emotions Control Us

The examples of Saul, Joab, Absalom, Ahithophel, and Rehoboam provide us with needed insight. We see in them the harm they did to themselves and others by letting negative feelings control their responses to their varied circumstances and to the Lord. From their examples, we learn to avoid the kinds of mistakes they made, and we see how important it is not to allow emotions such as pride, anger, and revenge deter us from the path of being faithful to the Lord.

Rather than give in to an unforgiving spirit, as did so many of the guys in our study, we can learn to bring the Gospel into all our relationships. As we appreciate what God has done for us—forgiving our many, many sins and giving us unending favor and life—such thoughts relieve our desire to strike back or harbor anger and bitterness in our hearts. Instead, we can develop the habit of quickly dealing with the feelings behind so many destructive tendencies by applying the Lord's truth to every situation.

If your life has not turned out the way you intended, take heart. As a follower of Jesus, you can know the Lord has a continuing purpose for your life, will never leave you or forsake you, loves you as a dear child, and will someday reward you for your service to Him. Please know that nothing can thwart His purposes for your life—both now and in eternity, when we will reign with Christ in His Kingdom.

Even if you have failed in some way, remember the example of John Mark. The Lord loves to forgive His wayward children, restore them, and then use them in ways that bless others.

Jesus sees what you are going through and loves you more dearly than you can imagine. Someday you'll see His gracious and loving purpose for all you endure—if not in this life, then surely in eternity.

Necessity of a Two-World Perspective

In Colossians 3:1–4, we read these words:

> If then you have been raised with Christ, seek the things that are
> above, where Christ is, seated at the right hand of God. Set your

minds on things that are above, not on things that are on earth. For you have died, and your life is hidden with Christ in God. When Christ who is your life appears, then you also will appear with him in glory.

These verses encapsulate the two-world perspective of the Apostle Paul. Our hope does not lie in the things of this world; it rests above in the heavenly realm and with the eternal inheritance that will be ours when Jesus comes for us before the start of the seven–year Tribulation on earth.

Now as never before since the time Jesus walked among us, we must fix our hope on His appearing. Lives dedicated to pursuing wealth, influence, and popularity will end in great loss much sooner than what happened to the bad guys in this study.

Life rarely, if ever, makes sense if we look at it solely through the prism of our short years on the earth. That's why we need a biblical, two-world perspective that values eternal realities above earthly aspirations.

How do we make sense of the tragedies that come our way or impossible circumstances to which we see no end? Sadly, many believers also put all their hopes in what they can gain from this life, but when afflictions start taking a heavy toll, they fall into despair and doubt. Such are the perils of the kind of one-world outlook that characterized the men in our study.

So, take heart, even if life hasn't worked out as you thought it would. A much higher hand is working all things for your good (Romans 8:28), both for now and for eternity. The God who created the heavens and the earth remains in charge of your destiny—now and forever. Take heart, weary saint: *No one can thwart the least of His plans for us.*

Those immersed in the culture of today might believe they can cancel God's ways, but in the end He will have the last word both for His children and for this Christ-rejecting world.

ABOUT THE AUTHOR

Jonathan C. Brentner is an author, blogger, Bible teacher, and retired financial analyst. Through his writing, he reaches tens of thousands each month with his perspectives on biblical prophecy via his website: www. jonathanbrentner.com.

Jonathan has a BA in biblical studies from John Brown University along with an MDiv degree from Talbot Theological Seminary. After seminary, he worked one year for the Lockman Foundation assisting in the development of the *New American Standard Exhaustive Concordance*. His time at the Foundation consisted of matching English words in the New American Standard Bible with their counterparts in the Hebrew and Aramaic text of the Old Testament.

He was a pastor for six years before pursuing an MBA degree at the University of Iowa, which led to a lengthy career as a financial analyst at a large corporation. He retired in 2016 to begin a full-time writing ministry.

Jonathan and his charming wife, Ruth, reside in Roscoe, Illinois. Together they have five children and a dozen grandchildren scattered about Wisconsin, Iowa, Texas, and Illinois.

NOTES

Introduction
1. John Eldredge, *Waking the Dead* (Nashville: Thomas Nelson, 2003), 96.
2. Ibid., 97.
3. David Fiorazo, *Canceling Christianity* (Warrenton, VA: Freiling Publishing, 2021) pp. x, xii.

Chapter 3: Joab
4. Alexander Pan, "6 Tiny Mistakes That Shaped Huge Parts of Modern History," Cracked.com, January 28, 2015, www.cracked.com/article_22044_6–tiny–mistakes–that–changed–course–history.html.
5. C. P. Gray, "Joab," in *Zondervan Pictorial Encyclopedia of the Bible*, ed. Merrill C. Tenney (Grand Rapids: Zondervan, 1977), 3:597.

Chapter 4: Absalom
6. "Danger of Bitterness," *Preaching Today*, accessed November 9, 2017, www.preachingtoday.com/illustrations/2000/october/12680.html. Used by permission.
7. This quote is often attributed to Margaret Stunt of the Hillsong Church in Australia, but it has been repeated by so many in the Christian community that its exact origin is difficult to determine.

203

Chapter 6: Rehoboam

8. Amy Morin, "5 Phrases That Signal You're About to Make a Bad Decision," *Forbes.com*, July 1, 2015, www.forbes.com/sites/amymorin/2015/07/01/5–phrases–that–signal–youre–about–to–make–a–bad–decision/#6efb70bf595d.
9. Ibid.

Chapter 7: Gehazi

10. J. I. Packer, *Hot Tub Religion* (Wheaton, IL: Tyndale House, 1987), 74.

Chapter 9: Eli

11. Martin Luther, quoted in Roland Bainton, *Here I Stand* (Nashville: Abingdon Press, 1950), 185.
12. Ibid.

Chapter 10: Diotrephes

13. Abraham Lincoln, quoted in Russell Razzaque, "Learning Humility from Lincoln," *Psychology Today*, April 10, 2012, www.psychologytoday.com/blog/political–intelligence/201204/learning–humility–lincoln.
14. Ibid.
15. Edwin Stanton, quoted in ibid.
16. Max Lucado, *In the Eye of the Storm* (Dallas: Word, 1991), 153.

Chapter 11: Asa

17. Charles Spurgeon, "A Lesson from the Life of King Asa," *Spurgeon's Sermons*, vol. 20, sermon 1152 (1874), www.ccel.org/ccel/spurgeon/sermons20.iii.html.
18. David Wilkerson, "Remembering Your Deliverances," *YouTube*, December 27, 2004, www.youtube.com/watch?v=F5LKuZUnd8o.

Chapter 12: Cain

19. John McCarthy, quoted by Warren W. Wiersbe, *Be Joyful* (Wheaton, IL: Victor Books, 1974), 125.
20. J. I. Packer, *Knowing God* (Downers Grove, IL: InterVarsity Press, 1973), 37.

Chapter 13: John Mark
20. Winston Churchill, quoted in "Top 10 Commencement Speeches," *Time*, accessed November 25, 2017, http://content.time.com/time/specials/packages/article/0,28804,1898670_1898671_1898655,00.html.